"Making America Great Again?"

The Rise of Protestant Guns

Ben Johnson

First Edition 2017

ISBN-13: 978-1981498123

Printed by: CreateSpace, an Amazon.com company

Cover Design by: Ben Johnson

Pictures for front and back cover depiction are available in the public domain at:

By Unknown - http://www.iwcp.co.uk/news/news/an-isle-of-wight-fleet-review-of-a-very-different-kind-83124.aspx, Public Domain, https://commons.wikimedia.org/w/index.php?curid=284027

By John Dee - British Museum, MS Sloane 3188, 16th cent., Public Domain, https://commons.wikimedia.org/w/index.php?curid=5517139

Public Domain, https://commons.wikimedia.org/w/index.php?curid=1383858

Printed in the United States of America

Questions and comments may be submitted by email to:

protestantguns@yahoo.com **or at facebook/protestant guns**

Contents

Preface

Throughout this past year's election, Donald Trump and the Republicans often used the phrase "make America great again" in their pursuit of the presidency. The election was a close one by popular vote, although Trump's electoral vote gave him the victory.

Our country seems to be split on this notion of a "Great America." Some view this country's history as a series of "miracles" or "luck" in which our country was propelled to a dominant position on the world's stage…and this being good. Others view our position on the world's stage as a manipulative oppression by our leaders throughout history, made up of mostly "Christian" elitists, and this of course…being a bad thing.

How can a nation, being only about 5% of the world's population, exert such dominance?

I have often pondered our position, have studied the matter over the years and now, more than ever, I believe it is time to share my discoveries to set the matter straight.

Although I am not a scholar in any of these subjects I will entertain, that is not as important as the missing links I will write about to help us figure out if this truly is a "Great America."

This book may seem politically motivated, but I assure the reader that this book is not written on behalf of any party affiliation, as I am registered as an independent voter. I don't prescribe to any specific party, and prefer to look at each candidate individually when it comes time to vote.

Most of the information in this book is easily accessible through sources such as Wikipedia and Google. Discussions involving general knowledge are cited only in regard to the source article. For a more in-depth look into a subject, please refer to the footnotes or references listed in the sources.

Finally, I urge the reader to stay with the discussions within this book, as uncomfortable as it might get, so you are able to ponder the end thesis. Although I am not seeking to "convert" the reader on any of my specific topics, I do hope for a softening and better understanding of America's position in the world. So...fasten your seatbelts, and let's take a ride into Pre-Renaissance Europe, where we can solve some of these mysteries!

Chapter One

"...a bloody and treacherous religion."

The year was 1572, August, and it was unusually hot in Paris. The queen, Catherine of Medici, had made recent concessions to the Huguenots to help quell what was known as the 30-year religious wars that were happening in France during this time. The Huguenot leader, Admiral Coligny was reestablished at the queen's court to ease tensions between Catholics and Protestants throughout the countryside.[1]

A controversial wedding was about to take place, the queen's daughter, Margaret, a Catholic, was about to marry the Protestant Charles the IX (future king of France). Tensions were high in Catholic Paris, as most of the population was against the marriage. They were disgusted that Protestants had even gathered in the

---

[1] https://en.wikipedia.org/wiki/St._Bartholomew%27s_Day_massa cre

city to attend the wedding. Admiral Coligny was also in attendance as a member of the queen's court.

Historians are not sure of Catherine's true intentions but, regardless, history was about to change the landscape of Europe forever. A few days after the wedding during the festivities, an assassination attempt was made on Coligny's life, in which he was severely wounded. As the Huguenot leaders learned of the attempt, small riots began to break out throughout Paris. Most Huguenots accused Catherine of Medici of orchestrating the attack, using her daughter's own wedding as a device.

A few more days after the assassination attempt, and upon seeing the unrest in Paris, the royal court advised the queen to kill the other Huguenot leaders in the city to prevent a possible military offensive on the city. This post-wedding plan was carried out, including the killing of the admiral. This was depicted in Francois Dubois' famous painting of the tower scene, where the admiral's body was thrown out the tower window.[2] The fighting in Paris continued for months and spilled into the countryside, amassing the largest number of casualties seen within France's religious wars. Historians have estimated as many as 30,000 people were killed, the majority being Protestants.

Religious wars were breaking out all over Europe during this time, so what made this one unique? It was a matter of attendance- many heads of state were invited to the wedding, and this included England's ambassador to Queen Elizabeth I, Francis Walsingham, who barely escaped France with his life.

Walsingham was a key figure in Elizabeth's court, along with Baron William Cecil, making up what I would call the "triumvirate," which included the queen herself. The British, during that time, referred to Walsingham as the queen's spymaster, who always seemed a step

---

[2]

https://en.wikipedia.org/wiki/St._Bartholomew%27s_Day_massa cre#/media/Francois_Dubois_001.jpg ahead of perilous situations and assassination attempts on the queen. He was most notoriously known for foiling the Throckmorton plot of 1583, in which attempts were made to replace Queen Elizabeth with Mary, Queen of Scots.[3]

Upon arriving back in England after surviving what became known as the St. Bartholomew's Day Massacre, Walsingham's resolve was clear. His brother-in-law summarized his zeal best when he said:

"I think it time and more than time for us to awake out of our dead sleep, and take heed lest like mischief as has already overwhelmed the brethren and neighbours in France and Flanders embrace us which be left in such sort as we shall not be able to escape."[4]

I have come to believe that this massacre was probably the tipping point in what became the Protestant domination that was yet to come. As one historian

---

[3] https://en.wikipedia.org/wiki/Francis_Walsingham

[4] Cooper, John (2011) The Queen's Agent: Francis Walsingham at the Court of Elizabeth I. London: Faber & Faber. p 80

described it, Catholicism was now defined by Elizabethan court as a "...bloody and treacherous religion" that must be stopped.[5]

The triumvirate was determined to end the Catholic oppression of Protestants that was happening throughout Europe, particularly the northern kingdoms. Part of this oppression had to do with who controlled the seas, as part of commerce and the gaining of wealth and territories through exploration. So, what does this have to do with America?

Without Protestant domination of the seas, there would have been no Protestant colonization of America, and no establishment of the "providential" republic of this country. When I say providential, I refer to the firm belief held by our forefathers that our nation's principles were established by God, through

---

[5] Chadwick, Henry; Evans, G. R. (1987). Atlas of the Christian church. London: Macmillan. p. 113.

man, for the sake of the majority in expense of the few.[6]

And why did I note a Protestant colonization? That is a matter of significance that I will discuss more in the next chapter. The fact is that America could have been colonized by any nation of beliefs, or even remained in the hands of the Native Americans, but the Protestant colonization by Northern Europeans somehow became the key.

At this point, some of you may view "colonization" as a negative force of domination between nations, or even a culture breaker. Whether you view it as favorable or unfavorable, my attempt is not to argue about colonization, but to accept it as a basic tenet of society. Colonization has been occurring throughout history in all parts of the world, as populations grow.

---

[6] Guyatt, Nicholas (2007-07-23). Providence and the Invention of the United States, 1607–1876. Cambridge University Press.

Look at, for example, China's recent colonization of Tibet, or Russia's colonization of Siberia in the 16th and 17th century. Even in our own country, there was the colonization of the Calusa in Florida, first by the Spanish, and then the Creeks.[7] These are just a small sampling of colonization efforts that got us to where we are now. In other words, the intercultural marriages and assimilation that occurred are what led to our own physical existence and cultural heritage we have today. To argue against colonization and assimilation would be to, in a sense, cease to exist.

So, the world is basically made up of various cultures whose populations grow, causing them to eventually fight, or make deals with other cultures for "more room." In basic terminology, this is the best way to define it. With the growth of the Protestant population in Europe during this time, and hostilities abounding between Catholics and Protestants, there was the need for more room.

---

[7] https://en.wikipedia.org/wiki/Calusa

Shortly after Walsinham's escape back to England, the queen made him principal secretary, a position later to become secretary of state. In his zeal for Protestantism, he worked hard as a spymaster, and foiled several Catholic-funded assassination attempts against the crown, such as the Throckmorton and the Babington plot.

Walsingham had developed one of the most extensive intelligence networks of the time, in which, by obtaining information from merchant ships, he had learned of Phillip II's plot to deploy the Spanish Armada to invade England.[8]

In July of 1588, the Armada made its move to secure the English Channel in an attempt to establish dominance in the region, and gain influence over Dutch regents. Under the leadership of Francis Drake, Lord Howard, and John Hawkins, the English succeeded in battle against the Armada in several skirmishes by

---

[8] https://en.wikipedia.org/wiki/Francis_Walsingham

wearing down their artillery, then forcing the fleet to retreat north up the English Channel, and reposition in the north Atlantic, west of the Shetland Isles.[9]

After more losses against the Royal Navy, the Armada began its retreat to Spain. Due to what I believe were the Armada's miscalculations of the Atlantic current and matters of longitude, along with stormy conditions, much of the fleet was lost along the rocky coast of Ireland in what was perceived as a divine defeat by Elizabethan England at the time.

The resulting effect may have given the Spanish a new respect for the Protestant cause which they believed was behind their defeat. Even Phillip II was quoted as saying: "I sent the Armada against men, not God's winds and waves."[10]

---

[9] https://en.wikipedia.org/wiki/Spanish_Armada

[10]

http://www.sparknotes.com/biography/elizabeth/section8.rhtml

The credit given to God was echoed in Queen Elizabeth's famous speech:

"My loving people, we have been persuaded by some that are careful of our safety, to take heed how we commit ourselves to armed multitudes for fear of treachery; but, I do assure you, I do not desire to live to distrust my faithful and loving people. Let tyrants fear, I have always so behaved myself, that under God I have placed my chiefest strength and safeguard in the loyal hearts and goodwill of my subjects; and, therefore, I am come amongst you as you see at this time, not for my recreation and disport, but being resolved, in the midst and heat of battle, to live or die amongst you all – to lay down for my God, and for my kingdoms, and for my people, my honour and my blood even in the dust.

I know I have the body of a weak and feeble woman; but I have the heart and stomach of a king – and of a King of England too, and think foul scorn that Parma or Spain, or any prince of Europe, should dare to invade the borders of my realm; to which, rather than any dishonor should grow by me, I myself will take up arms – I myself will be your general, judge, and rewarder of every one of your virtues in the field. I know already, for your forwardness, you have deserved rewards and crowns, and, we do assure you, on the word of a prince, they shall be duly paid you.

In the meantime, my lieutenant general shall be in my stead, than whom never prince commanded a more noble or worthy subject; not doubting but by your obedience to my general, by your concord in the camp, and your valour in the field, we shall shortly have a famous victory over those enemies of my God, of my kingdom, and of my people."[11]

Queen Elizabeth went as far as to call the Catholic Phillip II an "enemy of God." This pivotal victory towards the end of the 16th century is what led to

---

[11] Damrosh, David, et al. The Longman Anthology of British Literature, Volume 1B: The Early Modern Period. Third ed. New York: Pearson Longman, 2006.

British domination of the colonies established in America, by the mass immigration of Protestants in the 17th century. It seemed like God had directly "planned" this, almost by "divine intervention" as some at the time may have thought.

Most of us remember the basic explanation of this battle from our primary school years, as it is taught in most history classes. To the best of my memory, the teachers told us the reason the Armada lost was because "…their ships were too heavy from all their luxuries, and the British ships were faster, which enabled them to out-maneuver the Spanish."

Although this is partly true, this isn't the full story. The full story is not told to us to keep a certain political correctness within the school system, as not to show favoritism to one religion over another. But by avoiding the full story, one will not get a sense of the times as they are today.

Were Protestant colonists from Northern Europe truly meant to "take charge" of America, and "make America great?" The answer, I believe, is yes...seemingly by direct order from God Himself!

Enter a new player on this stage, John Dee.

Chapter Two

Special Revelation?

It seems that, every now and then, throughout history, a major player changes the course of mankind. Whether the reader believes this is an act of God is another matter, depending on the interpretation of the events at hand.

One example of this could be the Greek Plato, who laid the foundations of western philosophy and religion. Another example would be the French Napoleon, who gave us a common legal grounding through his development of civil law. But for the destiny of our own country's existence, God gave us John Dee.

John Dee, in my opinion, is actually greater than Napoleon, in the sense that the French forces could never penetrate British domination of the seas. He was also greater than Plato, in the sense that he expanded further into the sacred mysteries of God.

The triumvirate, Queen Elizabeth, William Cecil, and Francis Walsinham wouldn't be who they were without the acceptance of John Dee in their court. As a well-known Hermeticist, divinest, and alchemist, his acceptance to the royal court by the Protestant Queen Elizabeth puzzled me, until I studied that matter further.

Hermeticism is known as a belief in the writings of Hermes Trismegistus, which was commonly known among intellectuals in the 16th and 17th centuries. Although not accepted by mainstream Protestantism, some parallels between Hermeticism and Christianity exist.[12] Alchemy deals with the spiritual force behind substance, mostly attributed to the body and soul, although it also was the basis for attempting to turn lead into gold. This was a common practice in royal courts of Europe during this time, in their hopes to gain quick wealth.

---

[12] https://en.wikipedia.org/wiki/Hermeticism

Divination is known as the determination of supernatural purpose in seemingly unrelated objects or methods. A biblical example of this would be the casting of lots, which is a form of sortilege (or cleromancy). Every culture throughout history has always had some form of divination used in trying to determine future events.

As a Christian, I was wary of the methods John Dee used in his discoveries, but sometimes God has used similar methods to reveal His will. For example, in the Book of Numbers, God used Balaam to give a blessing to the Israelites, even though Balaam was, in a sense, a wizard. Also in the Book of Samuel, Saul consulted a medium in Endor to summon Samuel to determine the outcome of a battle between the Israelites and the Philistines.

John Dee devoted his life to the searching for and understanding of "pure verities," or divine forms that underlay the visible world, in an attempt to heal the rift between Catholic and Protestants. By recapturing the pure theology of the ancients, he explored the secret numbers of God, and influenced such notables as Thomas Diggs, Frances Bacon, Issac Newton, John Locke and Christopher Wren- all who have expanded upon his work.[13]

In his late twenties, and ahead of his time, he was invited to lecture on the geometry of Euclid in 1548 at the University of Paris, and by 1570, wrote *Mathematical Preface to Euclid's Elements*, which is still used in schools as a basis of geometry today. As an advisor in Queen Elizabeth's court from the 1550's through the 1570's, he was the first to coin the term "British Empire" ...even before there was a British Empire.[14]

In 1577, he wrote *General and Rare Memorials Pertayning to the Perfect Arte of Navigation*, and at the

---

[13] https://en.wikipedia.org/wiki/John_Dee

[14] Sherman, William Howard. John Dee: The Politics of Reading and Writing in the English Renaissance, p. 148. University of Massachusetts Press, 1995.

time became the leading expert in navigation, having trained most of the men behind England's voyages of discovery such as Humphrey Gilbert, Philip Sidney and Frances Drake. Drake's voyages and discoveries, among others, were ordered by Elizabeth to become Secrets of the Realm[15] due to what I believe are navigational discoveries of the time.

Prior to these navigational discoveries, John Dee wrote a book in 1564, *Monas Heiroglyphica* in which he derived mathematical relationships from sacred cubits existing in the Old Testament, giving England the geometric discoveries of his time. A full understanding of these mathematical relationships remains a mystery today, and without Dee's supplementary material, which was lost in the fire at Mortlake, it may still remain a mystery. Could he just be some random nutcase involved in writing quackery during his time?

---

[15] https://en.wikipedia.org/wiki/Francis_Drake

Well, when you look at his extensive library in Mortlake, England, the largest of its kind in his day, which was also presented to the queen to be the national library, it's hard to say he's a quack. Dee's library became a center of learning outside the universities, attracting many scholars of the time. He was even known to possess such rare books as the *Voynich Manuscript*, and the *Book of Soyga*.[16]

I believe the applications from his Book, *Monas Heiroglyphica*, and his other works on navigation and geometry are what gave Queen Elizabeth and her empire the resolve in making England's claim on the New World. She believed Dee had some sort of special revelation in his zeal for the colonization of America. Supposedly John Dee wrote *Monas* over a period of a few weeks while being in some kind of spiritual state, as if the words were being "dictated" to him. Elizabeth

---

[16]

http://www.joh.cam.ac.uk/library/special_collections/early_book s/pix/provenance/dee/dee.htm

believed this too, and it wasn't long before Dee became a trusted advisor to the queen's court.[17]

Let's go back to Dee's insistent claims of a "British Empire." There is another practice that Dee was familiar with, which furthered his commitment to the empire. He also practiced divination in the form of horoscopes, which he cast for Queen Elizabeth and Queen Mary. It was believed at the time that his divination had an effect on Queen Mary's health, in which he was brought to trial in the Star Chamber, an intellectual court of the time.

He won his case, and was exonerated by Edmund Bonner, the Bishop of London. Soon after Mary died, his calculations so impressed Elizabeth, that she allowed Dee to set her coronation date according to the stars, as approved by Robert Dudley, Earl of Leicester.[18]

---

[17] http://www.esotericarchives.com/dee/monad.htm

[18] Fell Smith, Charlotte (1909). John Dee: 1527–1608. London:

Some Protestants who knew of Dee's practices at the time, were wary of Dee's influence, and called it "the work of devils." Throughout the end of the 16th century, when laws made divination a punishable offense, Dee was let go from the royal court, and he sought to further gain knowledge from God through use of a scryer (medium), Edward Kelly.

The two traveled Europe during the late 16th century in an attempt to find patronage for their work with angelic communication, supposedly given through Kelly in the form of some kind of angelic language. Dee acted as the interpreter, and still sought to solve the mystery of "pure verities." Dee's direction was still clear- to advocate the expansion of the British Empire in Europe and the New World. Outside of Elizabeth's royal court during this time, he still was consulted in matters by the queen such as the Gregorian calendar change and other naval advancements.[19]

Constable and Company.

[19] https://en.wikipedia.org/wiki/Edward_Kelley

Some of his possessions of curved glass and other objects used for divination at the time of his court were most likely obtained from some of his masters, Gemma Friscus or Marcilio Ficino. Other notable students of Gemma Friscus were Gerardus Mercator and Abraham Ortelius, all of whom Dee maintained contact with.

Dee went a step further than his masters and was able to accurately calculate longitude by studying the advanced methods of the ancients, triangulation with use of these objects, and the application of biblical measurements. The leaders of the Voyages of Discovery were trained by Dee, with the results of these discoveries kept in secrecy.

I have reviewed these discoveries in Dee's *Monas* and found them quite fascinating, along with his esoteric mathematical principles. Later, in Isaac Newton's *Philosophiæ Naturalis Principia Mathematica*, Newton expanded further into the concept of *Prisca Sapientia*, sacred precepts Dee discovered almost a century earlier. These numerical discoveries derived from the Bible became the basis of mathematical formulas which calculate our physical laws. I can see how these discoveries are most likely the result of some kind of "special revelation."

A definition found in Wikipedia defines special revelation as "the belief that knowledge of God and of spiritual matters can be discovered through supernatural means, such as miracles or the scriptures, a disclosure of God's truth through means other than through man's reason."[20] Dee never had claimed to talk to Jesus himself, so that would rule out direct revelation, but his discoveries and the timing of these discoveries are a little more than coincidental.

The discussion of specific numerical theories derived from Dee's work is an esoteric topic beyond the scope of this book, but for the interested reader, one can

____

[20] https://en.wikipedia.org/wiki/Special_revelation

access most of John Dee's works online, or read commentaries of these works.

At this point, we see that 16th century England was being guided by some kind of "divine providence," propelling the British towards a dominant position in world culture.

But before we assume they were headed to be the most advanced, it is only fair to examine what the other cultures were doing during at the same time in the 16th century.

Chapter Three

The Dominant God

Before we can establish proof of God's blessings being with the Protestants, we must take a look at what was going on in other cultures at the time. Were other countries and cultures following a similar "renaissance" of knowledge and theories?

In no particular order, we'll first take a look at 16th-century Africa. During this time in history, the continent was divided into tribal regions, almost resembling the current states as they are today.

The Northern African states during this time were under the influence and control of Suleiman the Magnificent of the Ottoman Empire, and the Islamic kingdom. Large tribes such as the Almohad, Bornu and Kanem fell under the influence of Islamic caliphates either through commerce or occupation.[21] The people

---

[21] https://en.wikipedia.org/wiki/History_of_Africa

of Northern Africa were too busy making pilgrimages to the east, rather than seeking any land in the west.

The presence of Ottoman naval fleets in the Red Sea insured adherents with Islam, and were a big influence on Africa in the 16th century. The west side of Africa, controlled mainly by the Mali Empire, was split between Islamic adherents and tribal folk religions.[22]

There were also a considerable number of Christians throughout these regions, but during this time, they were either suppressed or infused with African traditional religions. Sometimes they were forced to convert to Islam. Some of the largest folk religions were that of the Akan, Yoruba, Bantu and the Zulu, predominant in the southern and central kingdoms.[23]

These folk religions, as common with others, have similar gods in the forms of the planets or elements, and also reference certain animals or plants in having

---

[22] https://en.wikipedia.org/wiki/Mali_Empire

[23] https://en.wikipedia.org/wiki/History_of_Africa

guidance and determination. Often these tribes would perform rituals to try to discover wisdom and predict the future. They certainly weren't trying to find wisdom from the scriptures or teachings of the Christians.

The religious groupings of 16th-century Africa are much different than the religious makeup of Africa today, with most of its adherents being either Christian or Islamic. But in the times of the 16th century, most Christians in Africa were either Catholic or Orthodox. There was only a small amount of Protestant Christians on the continent.[24]

In Eastern Asia during this time, the region was dominated by Ming dynastic culture, which incorporated Confucianism, Taoism and Buddhism. The dynasty was aware of the discoveries of the European continent through the established trade networks of the time, and by this, became aware of Christianity.

---

[24] https://en.wikipedia.org/wiki/Religion_in_Africa#endnote_n1

Along with the influence of trade, Rome was also sending missionaries to the region during the time, mostly Jesuits, who often disguised themselves as Confucianist scholars. They would often argue the discoveries of technology and science from the western world as reasons for conversion.[25]

The dynasty became increasingly hostile towards Christian ideas, which eventually led to the ban of Christianity, despite evidence of Christian practices (of the Nestorians) which predated the Ming Dynasty. With the population in firm grips of either Chinese folk religion or the others listed above, they were in no way seeking the God of the Protestants. They were, however, strengthening their navy and becoming a sea power and ruling authority in the pacific waterways.

It is ironic, that despite their rejection of Christianity, they still sought the navigational mastery of the British. This can be seen by the translations of Euclid's

---

[25] Wong, H.C. (1963), "China's Opposition to Western Science during Late Ming and Early Ch'ing", Isis, 54 (1): 29–49

Elements (and other western texts) into Chinese by Xu Guangqi, a convert in the high court of the Ming.[26] No doubt the Chinese were interested in the ways of the west, but for various reasons, the influence of western culture faded by the end of the Ming Dynasty.

Looking briefly into other populated areas during the 16th century such as Middle Asia, the region was at war with Babur, ruler of the Mughal dynasty (Islamic). This descendant of Genghis Kahn succeeded in suppressing the Hindu regions of modern day Afghanistan, Pakistan, India and Bangladesh.[27]

The region of Indonesia was also dominated by Islam in the 16th century, with the only Hindu holdout being Bali. Scholars generally agree that through the influence of Muslim traders to the region, the inhabitants were gradually converting to Islam. Although there were Christian missionaries in the

---

[26] https://en.wikipedia.org/wiki/Xu_Guangqi

[27] https://en.wikipedia.org/wiki/Babur

region during this time, they were not a dominating influence.

In Northern Asia, it was Ivan III who laid the groundwork for the Russian state as we know it today, by solidifying the Moscow Kremlin and defeating any remaining Mongol influence. He was followed by Ivan the IV ("Ivan the Terrible") who proclaimed himself to be the grand prince of Moscow.[28]

Although of Orthodox descent, Ivan IV envisioned himself as the divine leader, able to enact God's will in the form of the Tsar. He demanded full obedience for the surrounding vassal territories, leaving little room or time for a personal search for God.

Ironically, He befriended Queen Elizabeth I in an attempt to gain asylum in England if he ever needed such protection. During their discussions, the queen focused on trade, where Ivan was more concerned in

---

[28] https://en.wikipedia.org/wiki/Ivan_III_of_Russia

gaining a military alliance. No doubt he too heard of the marvels and successes of the British Navy.[29]

So, what about the rest of Europe, as far as their search for a personal relationship with God. Well...I am referring to, of course, Catholic controlled Europe.

A lot is written about Catholic Europe during the 16th century, so I will attempt to highlight only a few major events to set the scene. Towards the beginning of that century, papal authority was often falling in the hands of the richest, most powerful families that were often corrupt.

The Spanish-Italian house of Borgia produced Pope Alexander VI. The Borgia's were known to have committed many crimes, and were most famously known for murder by arsenic poisoning. They were

---

[29] "Russians in London: Government in exile". The Economist. 12 February 2016. Retrieved 12 February 2016.

often at war with the Medici family, the supposed masterminds of the St. Bartholomew's Day Massacre.[30]

Meanwhile there was a major challenge to Church authority, known as the Protestant Reformation. Martin Luther's challenge to the Vatican's Fifth Lateral Council was his "ninety-five theses." Huldrych Zwingli and John Calvin's also wrote arguments against the Church. The Acts of Supremacy by Henry the VIII was another main catalyst of this reformation, which had enabled a break with the Catholic church by establishing the Church of England.

Charles V of Spain, the Holy Roman Emperor, funded his campaigns through the Spanish explorers (known as Conquistadors) with help of enlisted Catholic clergy. Several big supporters of these conquests would include Dominicans, Jesuits and Franciscans such as Francis Xavier, Bartolomé de Las Casas, Eusebio Kino,

---

[30] https://en.wikipedia.org/wiki/House_of_Borgia

Juan de Palafox y Mendoza and Gaspar da Cruz.[31] The Protestant English were determined to thwart their territorial gains though British naval campaigns led by Elizabeth I. Both religious groups were jockeying for territories in the New World; the Catholics, for financial gains to benefit the Church, and the Protestants, to thwart the strengthening of the Catholic Church.

The more I studied this history, the more it became clear that there was not only a religious battle, but also a cultural battle. The French, Italian, and Spanish seemed to be more of one common ethnicity, and the British, Dutch, and German were more of another common ethnicity. Could it be that God was giving an "extra blessing" to a specific group of people?

If this were true, then it would not be because God loves one ethnicity over another, because God equally loves all ethnic groups and cultures.

---

[31] https://en.wikipedia.org/wiki/Conquistador

But could extra blessings occur as a result of past events as we've seen in Biblical History? The answer may be found by studying the roots of mankind.

Chapter Four

Table of Nations

In order to better examine America today, we need to go back a little further in time to discuss ethnicities and what is known as ethnonyms among people groups on the earth. Whether one is an evolutionist or creationist, both sides generally agree on a common ancestor for the roots of all people.

Even evolutionists agree that people didn't just "spring up" creating various ethnicities in various parts of the world. It is generally accepted that all people came from a single source, and the consensus seems to be that the origins of man come from the Mediterranean area. This takes into account fossil evidence, archaeological studies, epigraphical studies, and general ethnology.

The most well-known list of our early ancestry derives from Jewish history recorded by the Essenes in texts known as the Torah, and in further writings such as

Chronicles, found in the Bible. Although there is a slight difference between the lists in the Septuagint version as compared to the Masoretic text, the names are basically the same.

Other sources include Flavius Josephus' writings in *The Jews* and Hippolytus' writings in *Diamerismos*. Earlier sources include *Histories* by Herodotus, written in about 440 BC, which he gives us the Ionian world map. The following consensus of names are as listed in Wikipedia's "table of nations."[32]

The patriarch, Noah, supposedly had three sons, Shem, Ham and Japheth, and each son had a wife, along with Noah himself. These families are believed to have originated in the Mesopotamian area, or south east of the Mediterranean Sea.

Shem's descendants (Semites, which include Jews, Arabs, Eastern Indian and Western Asian) generally stayed in those territories. Some Semites migrated to

---

[32]https://en.wikipedia.org/wiki/Generations_of_Noah

Southern Europe over time, establishing the root cultures of the Greeks, Romans, and eventually the Spanish. Ham's descendants, known as Hamites, migrated west to Africa, founding tribes such as Cush, Put, Lud, and also Egypt, a name that remains unchanged to this day.

Noah supposedly migrated east and settled in the land area of Indonesia and China. There is actually a legend, investigated by the Jesuits in the 16th century, that the first Chinese emperor Yao was Noah himself.[33] These descendants later migrated northward, and eventually crossed the "land bridge" and became the North American Inuit.[34] These tribal people then migrated south and became known as the "American Indians," or "Native Americans," and may have married into other Asiatic groups who crossed the pacific, and

---

[33] Mungello, David E. (1989). Curious land: Jesuit accommodation and the origins of Sinology. University of Hawaii Press. pp. 179, 336–337.

[34] William G. Dean; Geoffrey J. Matthews (1998). Concise Historical Atlas of Canada. University of Toronto Press. p. 2

perhaps settled on this continent. This represents the general consensus among anthropologists and archaeologists, although many questions still remain.[35]

Finally, the descendants of Japheth migrated north of the Caucuses (mountain range north of Turkey) and settled in what today is known as Poland, Germany, the Netherlands, and Russia. They are also believed to be partly Scythian and "Magogian," descended from Magog the Japetite.[36] Although there was some intermarrying with Semites, the general population of the descendants of Japheth remained far north.

Some Semites that migrated towards the west of Turkey, stayed south of the Caucuses, intermingled with some of the Japhethites, and eventually became Spain, France and Italy. The Romans and Spanish supposedly descended from Kittim according to

---

[35] Goebel, Ted; Waters, Michael R.; O'Rourke, Dennis H. (2008). "The Late Pleistocene dispersal of modern humans in the Americas" (PDF). Science. 319 (5869): 1497–1502

[36] https://en.wikipedia.org/wiki/Gog_and_Magog

Hippolytus, and the Greeks from Javan, known as the Javanites.

The tribes that settled north of the Caucuses, or reached Northern Europe by sea, eventually became what are known as the Germanic tribes and Norsemen. Out of the Germanic tribes, we get the Anglo-Saxons, who eventually settled the British Isles. The Celts also settled the Isles, and they are a distinct people group supposedly descended from the Galatians, a tribal split from Magog, according to Hippolytus.[37]

The "Table of Nations" explanation of early ancestry is not agreed upon by every scholar, but I believe it is a good guide to where the people groups on the earth got their start. Ethnicities began with a basic family unit, who then became clans, who then became larger folk groups that eventually became nations. Nations can also emerge into one another, and become what are known as pan-ethnicities. Ethnic membership in

---

[37] https://books.google.com/books?id=N0FucWLGmS8C

Wikipedia is defined as having "...a shared cultural heritage, ancestry, origin myth, history, homeland, language or dialect, symbolic systems such as religion, mythology and ritual, cuisine, dressing style, art, and physical appearance."[38]

The groups covered in this chapter are only a simplified study of a few basic people groups that migrated throughout the earth. Most cultures have a distinct archaeological context, which support these claims and even give reference to their ancestral ethnonyms. So how does this relate to modern day America?

It is interesting to note a couple of verses in scripture, within the Torah itself, found in Genesis 9:20-27 (NASB):

20 Then Noah began farming and planted a vineyard. 21 He drank of the wine and became drunk, and uncovered himself inside his tent. 22 Ham, the father of Canaan, saw the nakedness of his father, and told

---

[38] https://en.wikipedia.org/wiki/Ethnic_group

his two brothers outside. 23 But Shem and Japheth took a garment and laid it upon both their shoulders and walked backward and covered the nakedness of their father; and their faces were turned away, so that they did not see their father's nakedness. 24 When Noah awoke from his wine, he knew what his youngest son had done to him. 25 So he said,

"Cursed be Canaan;

A servant of servants

He shall be to his brothers."

26 He also said,

"Blessed be the LORD,

The God of Shem;

And let Canaan be his servant.

27 "May God enlarge Japheth,

And let him dwell in the tents of Shem;

And let Canaan be his servant."

As we noted earlier, most of the sons of Ham migrated to what is known now as Africa, except for Canaan. The sons of Canaan stayed in the area of the Southern Levant, as the area is called today. It is often speculated that some of the sons of Shem migrated east into Asia, but most of them settled in the area known today as the Middle East.

This verse in Genesis may have more weight than some would think, and needs to be examined better. It seems like history has led us exactly to this point, and is being fulfilled according to this passage. For now, I'll let you ponder this verse, but I will come back to it in our final chapter.

Chapter Five

Old Ironsides

When Queen Elizabeth was in the waning years of her rule, a young Protestant leader was born, one who was to become one of the most controversial figures in British history. This, of course, was Oliver Cromwell, also known as "Old Ironsides."

Shortly after Queen Elizabeth's death, King James I from Scotland was invited by the queen's advisors to become king of England. He furthered the Protestant cause and became known in history for his commission of the King James Version of the Bible, which is still popular today. Under his rule, British occupation of the colonies began in the New World. His son, Charles I, succeeded James after his death in 1625.[39]

Charles held the view that the rule of a king was a "divine right" and often quarreled with parliament

---

[39] https://en.wikipedia.org/wiki/James_VI_and_I

over their attempts to limit his power. He became increasingly tyrannical in a sense by levying taxes without parliamentary consent. Coupled with his marriage to a French Catholic, and his attempt to anglicize government policy, many distrusted Charles; this lead to the English civil war between the royalist forces and the parliamentary forces.[40]

Cromwell was a relatively unknown figure in history up until his "spiritual awakening" in 1638, noted in a letter to one of his cousins. At this time, he became a dissenter, one who would later be called a Puritan. He set himself to be among "the congregation of the firstborn," meaning, the reformation had not been satisfactory because England was still living in sin due to lingering Catholic beliefs held by the Anglican Church.

Oliver Cromwell served in the early Parliament (1628-29) under Charles I, but it wasn't until the Parliament

---

[40] https://en.wikipedia.org/wiki/Charles_I_of_England

of 1640 to 1642 that Cromwell took action and became the controversial figure as he is known today.[41] What were the reasons for the controversy, and who is calling him controversial?

In reading much history about Oliver Cromwell, I find most judgments to be hostile towards Cromwell, unless it comes from a more fundamental Protestant analysis. While it is true that he put many innocent people to death during his military campaigns, in England, Scotland and Ireland, he saw these "innocents" as supporters of Royalist forces attempting to sabotage a firmly established Protestant core in England's commonwealth during the 17th century.

For example, let's say that France invaded the U.S., and in a certain town, several families chose to hide French fighters on their property, should we feel sympathy if by chance, both the American families and the French

---

[41] https://en.wikipedia.org/wiki/Oliver_Cromwell

fighters happen to get wiped out by a missile. Would I be considered cruel and heartless to say that these families "got what they deserved?"

Noticed how I used the word *families* to describe the people aiding the enemy. One could easily replace the word with *traitors* and the above sentence would perhaps make one feel less sympathetic for those who were killed by the missile. Simple word choice can put a negative spin on Cromwell and his rule of Great Britain during his time period, as several historians have done so.

The above example fits the precise definition of Cromwell's *Providentialism*, his view that God specifically "chose" certain people to direct the fate of nations, and that sometimes it is necessary for a few to suffer for the sake of many. British historian Nicholas Guyatt defines it more specifically, in that God judges the nations according to the virtues of its leaders, and each nation is meant to have a special role in the world's stage.[42] Cromwell's policies were fueled by religion rather than politics, and yes, it seems God was on his side.

After Cromwell overthrew the Royalist forces, beheaded Charles I, routed pro-Catholic forces in Scotland and Ireland, and resettled 60 percent of Catholic owned lands from Ireland, the commonwealth sought to make him "Lord Protector" of the British Isles. During the final years of Cromwell's rule, English Protestants experienced a peace like none other in British history. Cromwell remained humble in his position as Lord Protector and sought two main objectives: the healing and settling of a nation after years of civil war, accomplished by the authority of one man and a Parliament, and restoring the liberty of conscience and a godly spirit throughout the land.[43]

---

[42] Guyatt, Nicholas (2007-07-23). Providence and the Invention of the United States, 1607–1876. Cambridge University Press

[43] Hirst, Derek (1990). "The Lord Protector, 1653–8", in Morrill, p.173

As far as confiscation of Irish lands from Catholic families, many historians go so far to label this action genocide, or an ethnic cleansing of a foreign land. But one also could look at this as a victory over Catholic tyranny and then division of the spoils of war. Cromwell went so far as to say:

"I am persuaded that this is a righteous judgment of God upon these barbarous wretches, who have imbrued their hands in so much innocent blood and that it will tend to prevent the effusion of blood for the future, which are satisfactory grounds for such actions, which otherwise cannot but work remorse and regret."[44]

Either Cromwell was a genocidal maniac for making statements such as these, or he had some sort of military intelligence on the matter as a Member of Parliament in making his decisions. This statement

---

[44] Cromwell, Oliver (1846). Thomas Carlyle, ed. "Oliver Cromwell's letters and speeches, with elucidations". William H. Colyer. p. 128

almost fits the exact definition of Providentialism. The truth is as follows:

Ever since Henry the VIII and the Acts of Supremacy of 1534, The Holy Roman Emperor was funding a Catholic campaign against Protestantism through the Jesuits and Dominicans, to adherents in Northern Europe and the British Isles, especially Northern Ireland (the region least affected by Elizabeth I).[45] Charles I further was supporting these efforts by aligning Royalist forces (Anglican) with Catholic adherents which threatened to limit the freedoms of Protestants by imposing fines on Protestant worship, which as a result, funneled money back to Catholic Spain and France.[46]

During Charles' early reign, he failed to act to prevent what were known as the Irish Confederate Wars, or the robbing and beating of Protestant settlers from the earlier reigns of Henry VIII and Elizabeth I by the native

---

[45] Robinson, John J (1989) "Born in Blood; The Lost Secrets of Freemasonry", M. Evans p 291-304.

[46] https://en.wikipedia.org/wiki/Recusancy

Irish. The robbing and beatings ultimately led to killings, especially in the counties of Wexford and Ulster, where as many as 12,000 Protestant settlers were massacred.[47] In some cases, settlers were rounded up in meeting halls and the building was then torched, whereby they were burned alive. In another case known as the Portadown Massacre, as much as three hundred English families were marched onto a bridge and then forced to jump into the icy waters below. Those who survived were shot.[48]

The Irish Catholics then formed what was known as the Confederate, and were soon supported by Royalist forces, in hopes of Catholic concessions promised by Charles I. As history tells us, Confederate forces were defeated by Cromwell's New Model Army between the years of 1649-1653, and most of the Irish lands were

---

[47] Hull, Eleanor (1931). A History of Ireland, Chapter "The Rebellion of 1641–42"

[48] https://en.wikipedia.org/wiki/Portadown_massacre

resettled by Protestants.[49] Protestant dominance was here to stay, which also had its effect on England's Colonies in the New World.

During Cromwell's campaigns, he would often cite scripture for the reasons of his efforts. After the battle at Preston, his study of Psalms led him to say:

"...they that are implacable and will not leave troubling the land may be speedily destroyed out of the land."[50]

In several other letters to his generals, he gave Biblical examples as reasons for his campaigns, such as Gideon's defeat of the Midianites and other examples from passages in Isaiah. Cromwell viewed his victories as God's approval and his defeats to be a sign that God meant for him to take a different path.

Cromwell established the Commonwealth of 1649, but after a series of disputes and disagreements, the

---

[49] https://en.wikipedia.org/wiki/Irish_Confederate_Wars

[50] Simpson, James (2007) "Burning to Read" Belknap Press, p 20

Commonwealth elected to have Cromwell to become Lord Protector of England. Despite his "regicidal" title, he still maintained and called upon Parliament throughout the rest of his rule, noting that "Government by one man and Parliament is fundamental..."[51]

So, could all the events in England during this time be counted as "God's providence," as Cromwell would say? One would be hard-pressed to say it was "luck" or coincidence that was setting the course for Protestant domination. If John Dee and Elizabethan England gave Protestants the "brick and mortar," and Oliver Cromwell "built the wall," who then could we say, "completed the building?"

---

[51] Hirst, Derek (1990). "The Lord Protector, 1653–8", in Morrill, p.127

Chapter Six

The Glorious Revolution

This following chapter is not meant to be an exhaustive history of the 17th century, which you can find in any history book, but only the highlighting of a few points related to this subject. It is important to finish our discussion of Protestant Northern Europe before we can discuss the colonists in the New World.

By the end of Queen Elizabeth's reign, the northern kingdoms were increasingly awed by the successes of England's Protestant campaigns. New Christian theories and theologies, such as Calvinism, were winning Bohemian and Austrian princes to Protestantism, to the dismay of the Holy Roman Empire.

The main stronghold of Europe during this time was the Hapsburg dynasty, which asserted Catholic policy supported by an alliance with Spain. Although France was the largest Catholic state at this time, they held animosity for the Hapsburgs in fear that they were becoming too strong.

During the Reign of James I, Europe was plunged into the Thirty Years War by 1618, after the Holy Roman Emperor Ferdinand II declared Roman Catholicism must be uniformly practiced in his domains. The Protestant Union, consisting mostly of Lutherans and Calvinists, was formed out of fear of losing their rights of freedom of religion.[52]

For the next 30 years or so, alliances were made with Protestant Sweden, the Lutherans in Bohemia, the Dutch, parts of Austria, England, the French Huguenots, and a few other small Protestant territories in an attempt to end the Hapsburg rule, viewed as hostile to religious freedom. The final outcome was a treaty called the Peace of Westphalia in 1645, which was noted by historians to set the stage

---

[52] https://en.wikipedia.org/wiki/Protestant_Union

for sovereign nation-states. In that way, people would be subject to state rules over any religious power.[53]

In Great Britain, after the time of Oliver Cromwell, Charles II was quietly trying to restore the monarchy, which was favorable to Catholic Spain. More restrictions were being placed on the Protestant parliament during that time, which carried into James II rule in 1685. Both kings were attempting to make Parliament irrelevant, which meant the loss of the Protestant voice in the kingdom.

Then came what was known as the Glorious Revolution, or sometimes called the Bloodless Revolution. Some historians refer to it as the Glorious Invasion, because it really was the seizure of the British kingdom by the Dutch prince, William of Orange III. James II at the time, was making further alliances with France, and attempting to restore a Catholic dynasty

---

[53] https://en.wikipedia.org/wiki/Peace_of_Westphalia

on the island. Once again, the Protestant core of Great Britain was being threatened.

By the late 17th century, the Dutch fleet was mostly aligned with the English, and shared the same naval advancements and techniques. The English Parliamentarians were secretly arranging for William's invasion, and promised him the financial support. William overwhelmed the Royalist forces, and became the king of Great Britain in 1689, putting an end to any chance of Catholic rule once and for all.[54]

What came as a result of the Glorious Revolution was the Bill of Rights of 1689, a model that America was to use for its Bill of Rights 100 years later. Some of the main tenets of British rights were as follows:

- Royal authority was no longer allowed to suspend the law without consent of Parliament.
- Royal commission for ecclesiastical causes was to not be permitted.

---

[54] https://en.wikipedia.org/wiki/Glorious_Revolution

- Levying taxes without approval from Parliament was to be considered illegal.

- Subjects had the right to petition the king, and free speech could not be hindered.[55]

King James II's flight from England was considered to be an abdication of the throne. His policies were considered to be an "endeavor to subvert and extirpate the Protestant religion, and the laws and liberties of (the) kingdom." [56]About a year after the Bill of Rights, William III was declared king as laid out in the Coronation Oath Act of 1688. One of its provisions was to "maintain the laws of God, the true profession of the Gospel, and the Protestant Reformed faith established by law."[57]

---

[55] Williams, E. N. (1960). The Eighteenth-Century Constitution. 1688–1815. Cambridge University Press. p 28,29

[56] Kaiser, Fred P (1900) The World's Best Orations from the Earliest Period to the Present Time. The Werner Company. P. 2621

[57] Williams, E. N. (1960). The Eighteenth-Century Constitution.

One of the specific influences on the Bill of Rights was that of the Enlightenment. One may wonder how the liberalities of the Enlightenment could have such an effect in a time of such avid Providentialism. Well, my best guess is as follows:

From medieval times through the renaissance, kings and queens, generally Catholic, were constantly vying for power, and they often used a supernatural excuse as the cause of their actions. As discussed earlier, this was known as the "divine right of kings."[58] The Church, then, usually backed these actions. The Protestants were guilty of this also, by the very definition of Providentialism, although their backing came from a more personal sense.

By adding natural freedoms to this Bill of Rights, which could be seen in our physical reality, England made it "safe" for the commonwealth of man within their

---

1688–1815. Cambridge University Press.p.37-39

[58] https://en.wikipedia.org/wiki/Divine_right_of_kings

governance. The leading thinkers of the Enlightenment wanted to see the creation of laws based on the review and outcome of actual events rather than by spiritual directives. The Protestants had just defeated James II in the Glorious Revolution, so why would they make concessions that took away some of their spiritual causations?

My studies indicate that it was meant to put a final "block" on any Catholic or Anglican decree made by any royal authority which could then be used to limit the freedoms of true Christian thought and actions. By sticking to this Bill of Rights, the Catholic and Anglican churches would slowly lose their power and influence. As history shows, that is what has happened.

Before we leave this topic and cross the Atlantic, let's take a look briefly at three key leaders during the Enlightenment. As Thomas Jefferson once was quoted, "(Francis) Bacon, (John) Locke and (Isaac) Newton...I consider them as the three greatest men that have ever lived, without any exception, and as having laid the foundation of those superstructures which have been raised in the Physical and Moral sciences."[59]

Superstructures indeed, but let's see how far the modern view of these "superstructures" deviated from what was known as the norm. And let's see how much faith we've put in these superstructures over the intentions of the men who created them!

One of the main pre-enlightenment figures was Francis Bacon, also known as the father of the scientific method. Bacon was a Puritan who served as an advisor to Elizabeth I in her later years as Member of Parliament. He was in favor of the execution of Queen Mary, and also against the suppression of the Puritans. He wrote eloquent tracts in campaign against the oppression of Catholic Spain.[60]

---

[59] Wisley, John D (2011) "One Nation Under God?" An Evangelical Critique of Christian America. p.21

[60] https://en.wikipedia.org/wiki/Francis_Bacon

He was never "against God" as the liberal historians of today make him out to be. In fact, he was in awe of the discoveries of John Dee and worked with Francis Yates to find a reformation of "divine and human understanding" seeking to return the spirit of man as it was before the Fall. When I mention "the Fall," I am referring to the Biblical fall of man by separation from God due to man's sin.

As Francis Bacon discussed philosophy at the prominent Grey's Inn of London, it was noted by historians that he often met with Freemasons and Rosicrucians to discuss these philosophies, but he was never found in any membership. This may sound alarming to some, but the Freemasons, previously known as the "Knights Templar," were initially responsible for "setting the stage" of the Protestant movement.

Further advancing in Dee's footsteps was Isaac Newton, the man whose mathematical discoveries essentially started the industrial revolution by formulating the structure of classical mechanics. Widely known as a key figure in the scientific revolution, he laid out his formulas in his *Principia Mathmatica*. Amazingly he wrote *Principia* in the space of two years in following a much greater quest, the determination of the "end times" and Jesus' return to earth with his people.

As John Locke once said, "Mr. Newton is a really valuable man, not only for his wonderful skill in mathematics, but divinity also, and his great knowledge of the scriptures, wherein I know few his equals."[61] Newton actually wrote far more concerning theology, alchemy and philosophy than he wrote about the natural sciences.

In the words of historian David Flynn, "The revolution of science that Newton single-handedly achieved in Principia was primarily that the laws of motion and gravity, and the nature of space and time, had not

---

[61] Bourne, Henry Richard Fox (1876) The Life of John Locke, Vol 2. Harper and Brothers Pub. p.514

manifested apart from his immutable truths of the Bible…By his own words, the Bible was his source of inspiration for every theory that he conceived."[62]

Newton himself said "God gave the prophecies of the Old Testament, not to gratify men's curiosities by enabling them to foreknow things, but that after they were fulfilled they might be interpreted by the event; and His own Providence, not the Interpreters, be then manifested thereby to the world. For the event of things predicted many ages before, will then be a convincing argument that the world is governed by Providence."[63]

This is the same quest that John Dee sought approximately eighty years earlier, which was embraced by the English commonwealth. Could it be that God was advancing the English during this age of

---

[62] Flynn, David (2008) Temple the Center of Time. Anomalos Pub. House. p.16

[63] Isaac Newton (1988) The Prophecies of Daniel and the Apocalypse. Hyderabad, India Printland Pub. p.14

discovery? Did not God advance Israel when they wholeheartedly sought to reconcile with the Lord their God? Finally, let's take a brief look at one of the most influential leaders during the Enlightenment, John Locke.

Considered as the "father of liberalism," Locke was hardly a liberal in today's sense of the word. Being a staunch Puritan, he fought in the parliamentary forces against Charles II, and had to flee to the Netherlands for his involvement with the Rye House Plot, an assassination attempt on Charles II. After the Glorious Revolution, he served as an advisor to William III, and was a Member of Parliament for many years after.[64]

On one hand, it may seem liberal in that he came up with the idea of the "separation of church and state" due to his philosophical reasoning regarding epistemology, but this separation in no way had the same meaning as it does today. His definition was that

---

[64] https://en.wikipedia.org/wiki/John_Locke

government should not rule or make policy as a result of a "spiritual request" or commandment by any given ecclesiastical body, but instead, people should be governed by physical examples through a cause and effect relationship. More simply put, a government should not rule by spiritual revelation, but by physical, quantitative measures.

Locke wove this reasoning into the Bill of Rights of 1689, which put an end to any Catholic or Anglican decree of rule by divine appointment. Even though this could backfire on Protestant leaders too, they were more than willing to accept a suppression of their own spiritual fervor if it meant no more infiltrations by Catholic or Anglican influence. By the time of the Glorious Revolution, Protestants were tired of fighting. It was time for the age of invention to begin.

The words, *life, liberty and the pursuit of happiness* is taken directly from John Locke's Bill of Rights in our own Declaration of Independence.[65] Everybody should

---

[65] Becker, Carl. The Declaration of Independence: A Study in the

be free to believe and do what they want, according to Locke...well, not exactly.

The following is taken directly from Wikipedia in reference to Locke's beliefs:

"With regard to the Bible, Locke was very conservative. He retained the doctrine of the verbal inspiration of the Scriptures. The miracles were proofs of the divine nature of the biblical message. Locke was convinced that the entire content of the Bible was in agreement with human reason (The Reasonableness of Christianity, 1695). Although Locke was an advocate of tolerance, he urged the authorities not to tolerate atheism, because he thought the denial of God's existence would undermine the social order and lead to chaos. That excluded all atheistic varieties of philosophy and all attempts to deduce ethics and natural law from purely secular premises, for example,

---

History of Political Ideas. 1922. Available online from The Online Library of Liberty and Google Book Search. Revised edition New York: Vintage Books, 1970

man's 'autonomy or dignity or human flourishing.' In Locke's opinion, the cosmological argument was valid and proved God's existence. His political thought was based on 'a particular set of Protestant Christian assumptions.'"[66]

Well, so much for any argument defending atheism by reason of the separation of church and state. This denial of God's existence and its effects on society are precisely what is occurring today, and is far from the Enlightenment concepts of that time. Locke's followers, such as Voltaire, Rousseau and eventually Hume and Kant, continued to "water down" his concepts, which eventually lead to the Nihilist or Reconstructionist theories of today.

The results of the Glorious Revolution were that man could finally get the most out of life by having the liberty to be innovative and pursue happiness as a result of protections from religious tyranny.

____

[66] https://en.wikipedia.org/wiki/John_Locke

The most flourishing form of government emanated from the Protestants, and it was about to give birth to the Industrial Revolution. So...who were its leaders?

Chapter Seven

Industrial Revolution and Invention

Sometimes on any given workday, I may skip lunch in order to get things done. When I say, "skip lunch," I will at least stop by a convenient store, and refill my soda cup, and maybe get a bag of chips of some kind. Sometimes the task ahead of me is so much on my mind that it's more important to me to stay on the job, rather than take too much time for myself. I guess you could say that it bothers me that I'm not getting a task done fast enough.

It turns out, much to my amazement, that this is actually a character trait that goes hand in hand with what historians call the "Protestant work ethic" There are a handful of industrial revolution scholars who associate this trait with the dominance of Great Britain and the British colonies in America at the beginning of the Industrial Revolution. It is defined more specifically as:

"The Protestant work ethic, the Calvinist work ethic or the Puritan work ethic is a concept in theology, sociology, economics and history which emphasizes that hard work, discipline and frugality are a result of a person's subscription to the values espoused by the Protestant faith, particularly Calvinism."[67]

This term was first put forth in Max Weber's *The Protestant Ethic and Spirit of Capitalism* (1904). Calvinists (Puritans) of the time came to believe that it was possible to discern who was elect by observing their work ethic. This became the model of the time that families would strive for.[68]

If you look up "Industrial Revolution" in Wikipedia, the answer to the last chapter's question is within their first paragraph. Almost all historians agree that Great Britain and the colonies were this revolution's leaders,

---

[67] https://en.wikipedia.org/wiki/Protestant_work_ethic

[68] Weber, Max (2003) [First published 1905]. The Protestant Ethic and the Spirit of Capitalism. Translated by Parsons, Talcott. New York: Dover.

and many agree that it was due to this work ethic. It seems also that this ethic was a result of the discoveries a few centuries earlier. Here's a quick summary of what we know so far:

Due to the persecutions arising out of the Catholic Church throughout the 16th century, the Protestants finally chose to "fight back" and, in doing so, it seemed that God was surely on their side. England had defeated Catholic controlled Spain, as I believe, with the help of divine intervention through John Dee, advisor to Queen Elizabeth I. The secrets of navigation discovered by John Dee as mentioned previously, remained with the Royal Navy, which was the dominant force in the world until 20th century America.

As we briefly studied earlier, the other nations during this time period seemed to be doing anything other than seeking a personal relationship with God. Meanwhile, England was using its sea power to develop international trade, and making inroads in improving the technology of the world.

The world's greatest thinkers during the Industrial Revolution (most of who were Protestant) furthered their search into the sacred mysteries of God. This led them to propose many of the modern theories we ascribe to today. Through the 17th century, Protestant England won two more decisive victories, the restoration of the Parliament by Oliver Cromwell, and also the final defeat of Catholic and Anglican influences in the Glorious Revolution.

Great Britain was feeling "settled" by the end of the 17th century. Property rights and religious freedom led to individual confidence and productivity, and as mentioned earlier, became known as the Protestant work ethic. Northern Europe continued to lead in production through the 18th century, which was also shared by its satellite colonies in America.

The Industrial Revolution is a huge topic to tackle, in which I am unable cover in-depth, but I'd like to share a few highlights which got us to where we are today. The biggest advances were in machinery during this age, enabling man to increase production by moving from hand made products to machine made products. The ones who could make the most items in the shortest amount of time would become leaders in world commerce.

There were major advances in textile production with the invention of the power loom, which made cotton production forty times faster than the older methods known by hand. Also, the cotton gin enabled the removing of seed from the cotton plant, increasing efficiency by fifty times the previous rate.[69] Some of the biggest names in the development of these processes were John and Robert Kay, Lewis Paul, Samuel Crompton, Eli Whitney and James Hargreaves.

Soon after the Glorious Revolution, Thomas Savery invented the world's first steam-powered pump, which could be used in many industrial applications. Another version was invented by Thomas Newcomen, and both

---

[69] Woods, Robert (September 1, 2009). "A Turn of the Crank Started the Civil War." Mechanical Engineering

types of steam power were used through the 18th century. It wasn't until 1778 that James Watt, along with Matthew Boulton, came out with major improvements to the steam engine, increasing its efficiency and portability.[70]

Another big change was the use of the more efficient coal instead of wood burning in the use of metal and iron making. Coal could be heated to a much higher temperature in reverberatory furnaces known as cupolas. This was developed first by Clement Clerke, and later by Abraham Darby in what were known as blast furnaces. The Darby family continued to make inroads in iron production through the 18th century.[71]

Other important methods in the field of metallurgy were the rolling and puddling processes, invented by Henry Court. This increased iron bar and sheet production by fifteen times the previous known

---

[70] https://en.wikipedia.org/wiki/Stationary_steam_engine

[71] https://en.wikipedia.org/wiki/Reverberatory_furnace

methods. Better iron production reduced the cost of goods sold, which improved the quantities of hardware items used in various industries. Also, improved production of metals led to the advent of machine tools made by smiths and turners.[72] This was a key factor in the advancement of the British and American military, by the creation of interchangeable machined parts.

By the early 19th century, the machine industry became the leading industrial sector within the American economy, and greatly contributed to U.S. Department of War's use of precision made interchangeable weaponry.[73] After the time of American independence of 1776, it was priority that the country should maintain the highest quality

---

[72] https://en.wikipedia.org/wiki/Henry_Cort

[73] Hounshell, David A. (1984), From the American System to Mass Production, 1800-1932: The Development of Manufacturing Technology in the United States, Baltimore, Maryland: Johns Hopkins University Press

weapon standards in order to maintain the country's independence and freedoms.

It is important to note (again) that almost all of the leading developers during the time of the industrial revolution were of Northern European descent. Why wasn't this occurring in other parts of the world? Historians say the Napoleonic wars and social change hampered production in central Europe, leaving France to catch up to British production by the middle of the 19th century.

America also lagged behind in industrial advances through the 18th century, due to its agricultural base. The colonies existed more as resource providers to Great Britain, in which not much innovation was needed. It wasn't until after America's independence that it's industrial process "ramped up."

Japan was another country that took an interest in the Western developments of the industrial age. By 1871, Japan had sent a delegation of politicians to tour the West and see how Japan could become involved in modern innovations. This led to better schooling of the Japanese by the hiring of more than three thousand westerners to aid in the teaching of such things as mathematics, science and technology.[74]

As far as the rest of Asia, Africa, and other continents, the existing social status and cultural religions caused those people to take less interest in industrial change. Maybe this is partly due to the cultural focus on improving one's self through meditation and finding inner peace, rather than an encouragement of outward "works" as seen in Northern Europe. Historians Max Weber and David Landes believe that it was these differences in belief systems which dictated where the Industrial Revolution was to take place.[75]

In the next chapter, we will shift our attention to America, and focus on a few important highlights of the 20th century which put America on the forefront of

---

[74] https://en.wikipedia.org/wiki/Meiji_Restoration

[75] David S. Landes (1969). The Unbound Prometheus. Press Syndicate of the University of Cambridge. pp. 20–32

the world's stage. Much more can be said about the Industrial Revolution and the American Revolution, but we've discussed enough details to which I can address my points towards the end of this book. Again, this is not meant to be an exhaustive study of history, but rather a discussion of its makings, and how America came to be the dominant world power.

Chapter Eight

Three Main Events of the 20th Century

There obviously were many spectacular and not so spectacular events during the 20th century, but we will focus on three which were necessary for America to become the leading superpower of the world. But perhaps one would ask, is America truly leading the world? It depends on how you define the word "lead," but the emphasis from this point on will be from a military standpoint, because technology and innovation leads to security.

It might surprise you to know that our nation's leaders, up until World War II were generally against maintaining a standing army, or keeping a large military reserve. About a year before our independence, the Second Continental Congress assembled the continental army, navy and marine forces for the purposes of battling the British, and then were decommissioned after the treaty of Paris of 1784.[76]

Up until this point, we've been mostly touting the superiority of the British methods, so why then did they lose the War of Independence? Well, if you think about it, the British were actually fighting…the British! The colonies were essentially "Americanized British," trained in the methods of their former country. And they knew that they would never be able to defeat the British by sea, so the crux of the war occurred on land. As we all remember from our history classes in grade school, we were told that the Americans had the advantage on land due to their knowledge of the area and the change in fighting style.

The War of Independence lasted approximately six years until the British parliament voted to end the conflict, and recognize America as an independent sovereign country. Ironically, the Americans also had

---

[76] https://en.wikipedia.org/wiki/United_States_Armed_Forces

help from French and Spanish forces during the war, in return for small territorial grants. In other words, these Americanized Brits allied with the same countries they previously had fought with for centuries!

By the time World War I came around, the United States still did not have a large standing force, but managed to muster almost three million troops for the Allied cause. Woodrow Wilson at first wanted to avoid participation in the war, but our government was drawn in by German naval attacks against American ships. Wilson promoted enlistment as a "chance to end all wars by participating in this 'great war.'"[77]

There were advancements in warfare during this time, mostly seen in aviation techniques, tanks and types of heavy artillery that were used by the American, British, French and German forces. The Germans were more advanced in the field of artillery and U-boats (submarines), but the Allies soon found ways to

---

[77] Karp, Walter (1979), The Politics of War (1st ed.)

counteract these advantages. Due to the international cooperation of the Allied forces, the Central Powers (Germany, Austria, Hungary and parts of the Ottoman Empire) conceded defeat by 1919. The allies, mainly the "big four" (Britain, France, the United States and Italy), forced the acceptance of the boundaries of the European and Middle Eastern territories as we know them today.[78]

It wasn't until World War II that the United States was to become a leader in military strength and surpass Great Britain in military superiority. So…if God so favored the Protestant British throughout history, why then did His favoritism shift to the Americans? Well, by the mid-1900's Britain was increasingly becoming more secularized, meaning that their Protestant core was changing. The Protestants in Britain were becoming more ecumenical, while the American Protestants were staying true to the fundamentals of the Bible.

---

[78] https://en.wikipedia.org/wiki/World_War_I

One of the leading factors in the bolstering of the faith of America's leaders was our victory in World War II. Many in our core administration believed that God had favored our resolve to end Aryanism by defeating the Nazis, because it was viewed as an aberration of the truth. Adolf Hitler tried to "package" his Aryan message in a Christian manner, similar to the teaching style of the Catholic Church, which helped him gain the support of Christians who were unable to discern the difference.[79]

Shortly after the war, and within a few months after his presidency, Dwight Eisenhower dedicated his life to Christ following a baptism which took place at the National Presbyterian Church in Washington D.C. He credited God with the victories the United States had in World War II. This was to be the pattern of belief that would be held within the presidency, until the more liberal times of Bill Clinton.

---

[79] Rißmann, Michael (2001). Hitlers Gott. Vorsehungsglaube und Sendungsbewußtsein des deutschen Diktators (in German). Zürich München: Pendo p 201

One of the leading influences on the presidents from time of Truman to George Bush was Billy Graham, who was regarded by many of our more recent presidents as their spiritual advisor. Following on the heels of Chicago's D. L. Moody, Graham maintained strong Protestant core beliefs through these years, helping to keep our country Protestant-minded. Graham strongly opposed the campaign of John F. Kennedy, a Catholic, and worked "behind the scenes" with other Protestant leaders to thwart his candidacy. He was mostly seen in close association with Eisenhower and Lyndon Baines Johnson.

As a result of the Protestant resolve of the United States during that time, I believe that God allowed for three "key inventions" to fall into place for the United States, which would continue to keep these core Protestants as "world police" to this day. The term "world police," has a negative connotation to most...unless one is a Protestant, of course!

What this means is that America "holds the right" to judge other leaders in the world, in accordance with Biblical standards; and if it deems it necessary, change the situation if certain leaders are perceived as a threat to the world. In simple terms, if you are a world leader, and you want to "party" in expense of your country, you might be "punished" in some way, even if that means your death. We must look back to the definition of Providentialism, "...a few have to suffer for the sake of the many." And of course, those who are not Protestant are not going to want to be told what they can and cannot do! This is the crux of the secular dilemma which exists to this day.

Let's take a look at these three inventions, in order of their history. The first, as you might have guessed, would be atomic power. Much can be said on this topic, but we will only discuss it briefly.

Although German scientists theorized atomic power and detonation as early as 1938, its successful development, as history shows, went to the

Americans. This was primarily due to the availability of uranium ore located in Allied territories. The British were actually the most advanced in atomic development but lacked the resources for adequate production. This led to a Churchill-Roosevelt collaboration during the war in the development of a nuclear weapon.[80]

During the early 1940s, the race was on for the world's powers to create and control a successful nuclear detonation. The United States was the first to achieve this, with the testing of the Trinity "Gadget" in July of 1945.[81] A month later, targets were chosen in Japan and, as we all know, bombs were dropped on Hiroshima and Nagasaki, effectively ending the war a few days later.

Despite the controversy over atomic weapons that is still discussed today, The United States became the

---

[80] Gowing, Margaret (1964). Britain and Atomic Energy, 1935–1945. London: Macmillan Publishing. p 168-173

[81] https://en.wikipedia.org/wiki/Trinity_(nuclear_test)

leader in world affairs after these events. In August of 1945, Major General Leslie Groves estimated that at least six more bombs could be ready by the following months of September and October...if necessary.[82] This was no bluff; the uranium enrichment plants across the country had improved their methods of production and were adequately supplying Los Alamos, the bomb building headquarters, with the needed material.

The successful implementation of the atomic bomb was seen as "a gift from God" by our nation's leaders. Truman stated shortly after the bombing of Hiroshima "We may be grateful to Providence that the German atomic bomb project had failed, and the United States and its allies had spent nearly two billion on the greatest scientific gamble in history...and won."[83]

---

[82] "The Atomic Bomb and the End of World War II, A Collection of Primary Sources" (PDF). National Security Archive Electronic Briefing Book No. 162. George Washington University. August 13, 1945.

[83] "Statement by the President Announcing the Use of the A-Bomb at Hiroshima". Harry S. Truman Presidential Library and

The Americans had the biggest weapon, and the efficiency of uranium ore enrichment only improved following the war. Well, nobody likes the "big kid on the block," so this almost immediately led to the Cold War, the arms race between the United States and the Soviet Union. But in time, the United States seemingly had prevailed, so much so that the Soviet's organization underwent a formal dissolution in December of 1991.

A few years after World War II, three physicists, John Bardeen, Walter Brattain and William Shockey, working at AT&T Bell Labs invented the next greatest thing to secure our country's dominance, known as the transistor.[84] Better known as the point-contact transistor, some say this was the greatest invention of the 20th century, advancing us into the computer era and the modern times we know today.

Museum. August 6, 1945. Retrieved April 2, 2015.

[84] https://en.wikipedia.org/wiki/Transistor

The actual invention of the idea of a transistor was by the physicist Julius Edgar Lilienfeld in 1926, but production of high quality semiconductor materials was not possible at this time. Oskar Heil, a German inventor, also patented a similar version of the transistor in Europe in 1934.[85]

The invention was improved over the next several years, such as the invention of the bipolar junction transistors, field-effect transistors, high frequency transistors and silicone transistors. Transistors are used as switches and amplifiers, and have the advantage in being able to be mass produced. They also can be very small, in which they make up integrated circuits (microchips) which power and control many of the devices we use today.

Without microchips, the "smart" weaponry of the United States would not have been possible. These transistors, or chips, help guide missiles, determine

____

[85] https://en.wikipedia.org/wiki/History_of_the_transistor

targets, locate heat sources, send feedback, communicate with satellites and thus enable many of our systems to function with efficiency. The greater the efficiency in weaponry, the less cost in waste, better economies of scale, and the better total use per weapon.

Other countries were developing transistor technologies at about the same time in history as the United States, but America took the lead, primarily due to the excess of financial and economic resources following World War II. Many of the world's scientists and physicists were hired by American enterprises, which kept American chip technology in the forefront. One of the leading areas of chip production occurred in the Santa Clara Valley outside of San Francisco, also known as "Silicon Valley."[86]

Some points to note in relation to Silicon Valley's history would be technology advancements involving

---

[86] https://en.wikipedia.org/wiki/Silicon_Valley

the U. S. Navy in the Bay Area, U. S. Department of Defense spending, and the development of Stanford University's successful research tech lab, known as the Stanford Research Institute (SRI International).[87] These entities shared common goals in the development of the national security of the United States.

Shortly after the U. S. Navy moved their airfield operations to San Diego, the National Advisory Committee for Aeronautics took over operations located on Moffett Field, adjacent to Silicon Valley. This committee eventually transformed into NASA, which was signed into existence by Dwight D Eisenhower in 1958.[88]

The creation of a federally funded space program leads to the third invention, or should I say innovation,

---

[87] Castells, Manuel (2011). The Rise of the Network Society. John Wiley & Sons. p. 52.

[88]

https://en.wikipedia.org/wiki/National_Advisory_Committee_for_Aeronautics

which helped propel the United States to global dominance. This innovation would become the United States space program. I can't call it an "invention" in this case because the Soviets were the first to successfully orbit an artificial earth satellite, which was known as Sputnik 1. The Americans weren't totally caught by surprise though, because the U. S. Army's Ballistic Missile Agency had a rocket ready to put into orbit a satellite in 1956, almost a year earlier than the Russians, but this project had been delayed.[89]

In a way, the successful orbiting of Sputnik 1 enabled the United States to gain valuable information about space density and the transmitting of signals through the ionosphere. The events of Sputnik were perceived by Americans to be a "falling behind" the Russians in what became known as the "Space Race." President Eisenhower was well aware of Russian technology and developments through use of spy planes during the Cold War era. To further establish the United Sates

---

[89] https://en.wikipedia.org/wiki/Space_Race

foothold in space technology, another research agency alongside NASA was commissioned by Eisenhower in 1958, known today as DARPA (Defense Advanced Research Projects Agency).[90]

Eisenhower also contracted with Fairchild Semiconductor in Silicon Valley, the country's first transistor manufacturers, to help advance the U.S. space program.[91] Within a decade, the United States became the leader in space technology, with several working satellites in orbit and substantial improvements to inter-continental ballistic missiles (ICBM's).

Throughout the Cold War, estimates were often given to the public over what was known as the "missile gap;" the difference in missile stockpiles between the U.S. and Soviet Union. There was propaganda on both sides, but by the 1970s it was concluded that the

---

[90] https://en.wikipedia.org/wiki/DARPA

[91] "Timeline.Silicon Valley.American Experience.WGBH — PBS". American Experience. Retrieved 19 April 2015

United States had a six to one advantage in workable ICBM's, which clearly gave us the advantage.[92]

The "Cold War" was the name given to describe the preparations for a possible war between the two superpowers, the United States and its allies, and the Soviet Union and its allies. This was fueled by an armament race and military build-up on both sides, occurring after the end of World War II. The dates of this "war" vary among historians, but most consider its beginnings at the time of the announcement of the Truman Doctrine in 1947 to about the time of the Soviet reorganization in 1991.

The Truman Doctrine, along with the formation of NATO about two years later, was to be United States policy for the years to come. The leadership of the United States during this time was predominately Christian, and they viewed Communism to be a threat to the freedoms of religion around the world. It

---

[92] https://en.wikipedia.org/wiki/Missile_gap

became imperative for the United States to support satellite nations around the world, either militarily or financially, to combat Communist influence and aggression.

There were several smaller wars following World War II, mainly as a result of the influences of Communist Russia and China, although the two have not always been aligned in Marxist theory.[93] The biggest conflicts would be the Korean and Vietnam wars, in which the United States involvement was to prevent the further spread of Communism.

There is much debate and historical opinion over these conflicts, and the role of the United States Armed Forces, post-World War II, so the next chapter will be devoted to an ideological debate of what I call "the two main governing systems in the world." But let's begin the next chapter with something mentioned

---

[93] https://en.wikipedia.org/wiki/Sino-Soviet_split

early in this book, more specifically, the bold statement of my last paragraph in chapter one.

Chapter Nine

The American Military

and the "Protestant Cause"

If you examine our current military at home and abroad, one could easily say that America has become great. And by great, I mean our military gives us an authoritative position in the world, and makes us the driving force behind world affairs. Again, it all started from Northern European colonists, seeking Protestant freedom.

At roughly half a trillion dollars per year, the United States expenditures and funding account for forty percent of the world's total expenditures on military operations. We currently boast the largest air force in the world, and our navy has the second largest air force operating throughout the world. For pre-emptive and security reasons, the United States maintains nearly eight hundred bases abroad in one hundred fifty countries around the world.[94]

Approximately 400,000 forces are deployed overseas, with slightly over a million stationed domestically, who are currently in active duty. Although we don't have the largest military in terms of personnel, we are the most advanced in terms of technology and strategy. The United States is listed as having the highest "power projection," a term used to show a nation's ability to react and control a situation outside its domestic territory. Our power projection achievements came as a result of adapting British techniques in the 19th century, and using examples of their successes to influence our overseas military spending.[95]

Modeling in the same ways that the British secured their trade routes in the 17th and 18th centuries, the

---

[94] https://en.wikipedia.org/wiki/United_States_Armed_Forces

[95] https://en.wikipedia.org/wiki/Power_projection

United States secures the trade and commerce of the world today.[96] Some side benefits include better security for the monetary systems of the world, better ease and safety of world travel, and a better surveillance and deterrence of world crime. There are many benefits that Americans don't even realize they are enjoying, due to the Protestant concepts contained within the United States military.

Now let's discuss and theorize what would happen if the strength and technologies of our military were in the hands of a different (non-NATO) country...how would this affect the world economy and stabilization? Before we discuss this further, we first need to analyze a few of the main government ideologies throughout the world, and the belief systems that maintain them.

First, we'll take a look at our biggest rival, Communism, utilized mainly by Russia and China. After World War II, Russia and China were not necessarily aligned with

---

[96] https://en.wikipedia.org/wiki/Gunboat_diplomacy

their view of Communism. Shortly after the war, Stalin signed a treaty with Mao offering military aid and monetary assistance over a 30-year period to help China defeat nationalist uprisings against Communism within their own state.[97]

After Stalin's death in 1953, Khruschchev adopted a policy of tolerance toward capitalist nations, a move that Mao called Marxist revisionism. Mao took a more hardline approach to Communistic rule, which eventually led to the Sino-Soviet split of the 1960s, which caused both Russia and China to align different satellite countries to their brand of Communism.[98]

Despite their differences, both brands of Communism rejected the religious freedoms of the west, and sought to establish atheism as the core belief of the people. Communism by itself does not assign any preference for any religion, but atheism was

---

[97] https://en.wikipedia.org/wiki/Sino-Soviet_Treaty_of_Friendship,_Alliance_and_Mutual_Assistance

[98] https://en.wikipedia.org/wiki/Sino-Soviet_split

"attached" to Communism by Karl Marx and Fredric Engels, and by other thinkers of the 19th century.

You may be surprised to know that a simple form of Communism was utilized by the apostles and the early church after the resurrection of Jesus, to help ensure the resources of believers. In Acts 4:32 and 34 (NASB), the apostle Paul notes:

"32 And the congregation of those who believed were of one heart and soul; and not one of them claimed that anything belonged to him was his own, but all things were common property to them…34 for there was not a needy person among them, for all who were owners of land or houses would sell them and bring the proceeds of the sales and lay them at the apostles' feet, and they would be distributed to each as any had need."

This sort of "Christian Communism" took place within the imperialistic times of the Roman occupation of Israel. Even though Communism is not the mainstream philosophy derived from Christianity, there actually are

Christian Communist groups throughout the world today who adhere to such a structure.[99]

Karl Marx was partly influenced by the German philosopher Ludwig Feuerbach, among others, who held the position that religion was simply "made up" to alleviate the class struggle and make the poor accept their poverty as a part of God's plan. Frederic Engels took a similar stance, and the two philosophers included these theories in their most notable work, the *Communist Manifesto*.[100]

They thought that eliminating religion, which was considered to be a "waste of time," would make the worker more efficient and in turn, produce more output. Well...what Marx and Engels failed to realize was the blessings bestowed on the Protestants, which started centuries earlier, due to their Protestant work ethic, thereby allowing for the successes of the

---

[99] https://en.wikipedia.org/wiki/Christian_communism

[100] https://en.wikipedia.org/wiki/Karl_Marx

Industrial Revolution. How could Marx and Engels ignore these successes? Is the working class really "at the expense" of the capitalists?

One could look at this "elimination of religion" associated with communism in many ways. Upon studying Marx, I noticed almost all of his influences were either German or French, and ironically, they were the two countries that were falling behind in innovation to that of the British and Northern European industries. Could there have been jealousy among these "great thinkers," who came out of these lagging nations? Could this have been a plot by the revolutionist thinkers to weaken or overthrow the leading nations of the industrial revolution?

But despite its origins, the Communist front was solidified out of the vacuum of World War II, and so began the two competing world systems which exist today- Capitalism and Communism. Let's pretend first, that Russia and/or China had achieved nuclear superiority after the war, had the leading military production techniques from the Industrial Revolution, and had its own "Silicon Valley," which had attracted scientists and investors from around the world. Assume they had the military build-up, and the United States military (after the war) was relatively small, and no longer a world influence. How would either Russia or China then use their superior and influential fighting forces?

According to those German revolutionists, it would be most beneficial if the whole world would realize the "efficiencies" of a Communistic society, so Russia or China would not have maintained diplomacy with other countries for long. The Communist line in Europe would probably not have been drawn, and there would have been a gradual takeover of Europe.

In the Asiatic countries, Communist forces would have easily marched into southern Korea and Vietnam, and soon all the smaller southern Asian countries would have given way soon after. There would be some resistance from the Hindu nations such as India,

Bangladesh and Pakistan, but soon they would fall also. Most likely, Russia or China would collaborate and use a superior military force to eventually turn the world Communist.

Since we mentioned the Hindus in the last paragraph, let's theorize what would happen if the Hindu conglomerate of nations had the full military strength to that of the Americans after the war. It's hard to imagine the Hindus need to imperialize, so territorial gains would probably be slow, and a move to take over another nation would probably be only in response to hostilities against the Hindu people.

One thing that might have been different if Hindu leaders (Brahmin or Kshatriyas) had the superior military of the world, is that the caste system probably would have remained unchanged, and lower caste people would have continued to be oppressed. Part of the reason for caste system reform was due to diplomatic relations with the west after World War II, whereas India (the largest Hindu nation) adapted civil rights laws, such as the Untouchability (offences) Act of 1955 to alleviate the prejudices between the classes and create and equal opportunity work force.[101]

How would the spectrum of world power look if the Islamic countries had achieved military supremacy after the events of World War II? Given that the world's best oil supply comes from the Middle Eastern nations, those nations would have no shortage in resources to maintain a large, sophisticated military, and I'm sure Islamists would capitalize on that potential.

Despite which sect of Islam one might belong to, there are many verses in the Quran which allude to and support the "fighting of the infidels," or unbelievers. Some scholars believe this as a defense for Islamists in their region in case of an attack. Other scholars believe that because most verses occur during the time of

---

[101]

https://en.wikipedia.org/wiki/Scheduled_Caste_and_Scheduled_Tribe_(Prevention_of_Atrocities)_Act,_1989

Mohammed's occupation of Medina, with no threat of surrounding forces, that his words are directed offensively.

Some examples of this would be found in the Quran such as Sura 2:191-193; "And kill them (unbelievers) wherever you find them, and turn them out from where they have turned you out..." Sura 4:76 "Those who believe fight in the cause of Allah..." Sura 8:12 "I will cast terror into the hearts of those who disbelieve, therefore strike off their heads, and strike off every fingertip of them." There are many more verses similar to these throughout the Quran.

The Sunni's and Shi'is have differing views regarding these verses, and both have their own approach when dealing with outsiders. Superior weaponry in the hands of the more radical Shi'is, mainly Iran, would probably lead to a full-scale offensive in a short matter of time. The Sunni's would probably take a more diplomatic approach instead of a hostile takeover, but both forms of Islam would seek converts and force global taxation on those who remain unbelievers.

It seems today that some Islamic groups are on the offensive, trying to establish their culture and beliefs in regions that were never Islamic territories. It should be obvious that a superior military in the hands of the Islamist would lead to an eventual submittal to the tenets of Islam, rather than cultural tolerance and world trade.

Lastly, what would have happened if Protestant England fell to the Catholic Phillip II of Spain in 1588, and the Catholics had gained sea superiority? Let's theorize what would happen if a Catholic country, such as France, Spain, Italy or any South American country was given military superiority over the world.

The Catholic headquarters, the Vatican, maintains a small force known as the Pontifical Swiss Guard, kept mainly as a protection service for the Pope. Recruitment to this force is through a special agreement between the Holy See and Switzerland.[102] The garrison maintained by the Vatican is small, so instead of theorizing if this small militia was to have military superiority, we will take a brief look at a few countries that are largely of Catholic influence.

If either France or Spain was given military superiority on today's world stage, the military would probably be used mainly to secure monasteries and other Catholic outposts throughout the world. Although there may be no direct offensive, favoritism would be given to any country supporting or converting to the Catholic cause. I believe, that over a period of time, Spain or France would support a form of taxation based on use of their military security, whose proceeds would go to the Vatican, which in turn would funnel back to Spain or France. In other words, one could do well as a convert to Catholicism, and not so well to be "outside of the Church."

---

[102] https://en.wikipedia.org/wiki/Pontifical_Swiss_Guard

As far as any South American country goes, they would probably follow a similar pattern. Given a superior military, they would probably maintain some sort of form of dictatorship influenced by the Catholic Church within their countries, and conduct trade and levy taxes in a way that would benefit the Catholic Church. So basically, if any of these Catholic countries existed with military superiority, the Vatican would become even more wealthy within a short matter of time. Although Catholics are believers of the same Bible as the Protestants, exceedingly great wealth could lead to similar corruptions within the Church as occurred in the past. In regard to a Catholic/Protestant conflict, I believe history would most likely repeat itself, as in the times before the Glorious Revolution.

These examples given are not intended to single any one culture or religion out. In reality, all cultures take the "my way is best" attitude on the world stage; in fact, that's how we survive and carry on...its part of the pride of humanity. Protestants are guilty of this also, but I believe that the "my way is best" of the

Protestants is the "fairest" way for all the world cultures. Here are some reasons why:

Within about 10 or so years after World War II, the Protestant leaders of the United States could have at any time organized an offensive on any country, and most likely would have realized success. We could have pushed from North Vietnam into China at the time of the Vietnam War, but instead we chose diplomacy and established a military presence in South Vietnam. We also could have occupied Russia immediately after the war, given that they had been weakened by the German front, and we had achieved nuclear supremacy. General Patton's strategies had proved successful in rapid expansion into Germany, but Eisenhower redirected Patton's Third Army towards Prague.[103]

During the 1967 Six-Day War, or the Yom Kippur War of 1973, the United States could have easily "stepped

---

[103] https://en.wikipedia.org/wiki/George_S._Patton

in" and helped Israel take over Egypt, or perhaps invaded Jordan or Syria, but instead over time, we encouraged diplomatic relations between Israel and the surrounding Arab countries. During the Gulf War, the Americans at any time could have maneuvered forces into any other of the Arab territories, but instead they chose to stabilize Iraq and work with the Iraqi people to secure their region.

The tone of the American administration after World War II has generally been one of diplomacy. The United States has only acted upon aggressive fronts by other nations, not with intent of occupation, but with the intent of protection of cultures and freedoms. For example, although the Protestant core of our administration stands against Communism, the Islamic front and other smaller fascist regimes, we still are willing to conduct trade and help improve the standards of living of people in these countries. The hope would be that someday they can enjoy the freedoms we have, given by our Bill of Rights, based on Protestant concepts.

The reason I believe that this Protestant-founded country makes for the best "world police" is this: Pure Protestantism (although not always achieved) has the least amount of "contingencies" to that of any other world religion and belief system, so it requires the least amount of materialism to that of any other culture. In other words, every other religion hinges on the protection of some kind of location, temple, relic or leader, whereas the Protestant focuses only on the belief inside the individual, which requires no cost to the world, or expense of resources.

For example, the Communist (or atheist) form of protectionism is one of material goods and production. Because Communists believe that production without the "inefficiencies of religious belief" works best to maximize production for all people, then the surrounding countries with religious beliefs become a "threat" to the Communist, which then must be changed by an offensive front. As Marx States in *Theses on Feuerbach*, "...the philosophers have only interpreted the world, in various ways; the point however is to change it."

How "Protestant" is the United Sates today, and is this still a factor in the electoral and general vote? We are finally getting into modern politics, hence the title of this book. How does this current administration fit in the world today? As I learned in college, it is a mathematical improbability that statistics can lie, so let's take a look at a few statistics as we head into the current state of affairs of today.

Chapter Ten

Trump's Presidency and Current Events.

According to the United States Census Bureau and the Population Reference Bureau, the world's population is generally estimated at slightly over seven billion people. When one searches different databases to discover the proportions of world religions, the statistics generally follow this table:[104]

Christianity	2.2 billion (31.5%)
Islam	1.7 billion (23.2%)
Non-Religious	1.2 billion (16.3%)
Hinduism	1.1 billion (15.0%)
Buddhism	488 million (7.1%)
Folk Religions	400 million (5.5%)
Other	120 million (1.4%)

---

[104] https://en.wikipedia.org/wiki/Major_religious_groups

Christianity is defined as both Catholic and Protestant, and any other denominations that believe in the Judeo-Christian God of the Bible. Worldwide there are about 900 million Protestant adherents, which is about 12% of the world's population. As of 2015, Protestants made up almost 40% of the population in the United States, by far the majority religion.[105] Given a population of about 325 million, there are about 130 million Protestants in the United States, who make up roughly 2% of the total world population. Yet, they are the leading influence within our armed forces, which again, has the highest power ranking in the world.

Another interesting thing to note is that the non-religious are at approximately 16% of the world's population or make up roughly about two out of ten people. But what that means is that eight out of ten people believe in some kind of "higher power," or that some kind of "spiritual world" exists along with our

---

[105] https://en.wikipedia.org/wiki/History_of_religion_in_the_United_States#cite_note-gallup-5

own reality. This makes the atheist or unbeliever an overwhelming minority on the world's stage.

Often, I find that the non-religious unbelievers (atheists) who live in America, go out to coffee shops, restaurants or bars with each other, have their own TV shows they talk about, gravitate toward each other at work, and in a sense, form their own 'cliques." They swipe their credit cards to make purchases, order things online, safely drive from one place to another, call emergency services when needed...and forget to realize that all these possibilities are backed by the "unseen" Protestant military base of this country! And, although they think that they are the dominant view in these modern times...they are actually the minority.

The United States is backed by NATO, and is the leading influence within NATO. So, this is what I mean in the beginning of this book when I said that 2% of the world's population is, in effect, controlling, or "policing" the world, hence the sub-title of this book, "Protestant Guns."

A lot of liberals, or basically those who are not Protestant, think this is "not fair." Well, not fair to whom? As I sit here and write this as a Protestant Christian, it seems fair to me, but that's only because I see God working blessings through the leaders of those mentioned earlier to get us where we are now. Would I be able to sit here and give this same view as an Italian, Russian, German or citizen of any other culture?

It is the nature of man to want to be "the best." We want to go home to our women, look them in the eye, and say "I'm the best." And when this doesn't happen, the pride of man seeks to make it so. In other words, America is similar to the "biggest kid in the gym," and during a game of dodgeball, everybody else wants to get him!

America could also be likened to the Biblical "Goliath," whereas every other country is trying to be "David," and take Goliath out with a stone. But that's all they can do- throw stones. A "stone" in this case, can be defined as a liberal movement, a piece of "fake news," a terrorist attack, an organized protest or anything else to try to throw off the giant. But if any true war was waged on the giant, the other opponent knows that they would be crushed. Ironically, those trying to be like David, are not following the Biblical example of David at all, but are instead ineffective "copies." The real David succeeded in taking out the giant, because he truly was aligned with God.

To answer the question presented in the previous paragraph, let's pretend I was a Romanian, and I had come home from work one day, and my wife asks "...why is America doing better than us?" I would most likely show a look of disgust, become defensive, and say something like "Well, it's because they cheat...or, they are empowered by some kind of evil...or, it's just dumb luck!" But if this Romanian sat down and truly studied the history, maybe the words would change to "...wow, well I guess America did the right things at the right time, and well, we (meaning Romanians) didn't..."

This conversation leads into the final point of this book, and the answer I have realized over many years of reading, research and thoughts on this world we live in. This isn't just a quick thought I had while eating a cheeseburger and fries, daydreaming out the window on any given day! So, here it is...

Every culture's current status is due to either blessings or curses given by God, over the course of time. These blessings and curses have begun since the time of man, and act as an "invisible hand" in guiding a culture to their current state. Those cultures who can break generations of "bad habits" (as the British did in the 16th century), in an attempt to draw closer to God, are able to receive a blessing. A blessing can be defined as a gift of opportunities granted to a culture seeking to improve themselves by breaking bad habits. Likewise, a curse can be defined as a loss of opportunities and misdirection due to cultural pride and complacency within a certain country or region.

Maybe this idea has been thought of before, but has it really ever been put to the test? The non-believer or atheist would say either "...well, it's just luck with how events happen," or "...how a nation becomes powerful is just a manipulation by the rich who are in secret collusion." However, there is a problem with these two points of view.

Firstly, to use the word "luck" or "fate," implies a spiritual force influencing the material events in our everyday life. The origin of the words came from the middle ages, but it was first associated with the Roman goddess Fortuna. It is a word hijacked by non-believers to imply a science of chance.

The problem I have with the second statement is a little more detailed. Yes, I believe that it's true that groups of rich or well to do people have the ability to get together and collude to influence the masses or production. In other words, I believe in the presence and influence in what is known as "secret societies," but don't count them as the main guiding force of a nation.

Part of the problem is that many nations or cultures have their own secret societies, and some are actually in competition with each other. The leading factor of a nation's wealth is invention and ingenuity, which comes before collusion of individuals seeking to control it. And if one uses the Roman concept of "luck" in describing that invention, then one implies a spiritual force causing that luck.

Based on the historical summary in this book, it is clear that the group of people leading in inventions and theories were influenced and driven by the seeking of divine wisdom given by God. If there truly is a godly "force" out there, wouldn't that force "return the favor?" Based on the promises of God to protect His people in the Bible, it seems that God would show favoritism to those who believe.

So, in viewing the election results and other current events, I view Donald Trump's election to be sort of a

return to our nation's earlier principles of divine
Providence, as in the time of Dwight D. Eisenhower
after the war. Trump even seems to be following a
similar pattern.

If one recalls, Eisenhower became a Christian shortly
after his inauguration into the presidency, and sought
to put this country on the path to honor God. He is
responsible along with congress for adding the phrase
"in God we trust" on our paper currency and adding
the term "one nation, under God" in our pledge of
allegiance.[106] He also showed support for other
congressional and judicial measures such as the
approval of states "blue laws" and support for
containment of Communist (anti-Christian) ideas and
expansion.

During his campaign, Donald Trump promised to keep
the phrase "in God we trust" on our currency, along

---

[106] Federer, William J (1994) America's God and Country;
Encyclopedia of Quotations. Amerisearch, Inc. Pub. p 171,226

with "one nation, under God" in our pledge of allegiance.

No doubt Eisenhower understood the influence of God in the founding of our nation. In 1954, he stated: "The purpose of a devout and united people was set forth in the pages of the Bible… (1) to live in freedom (2) to work in a prosperous land…and (3) to obey the commandments of God…This Biblical story of the Promised land inspired the founders of America. It continues to inspire us…"[107]

In the adding of the phrase "under God" into our pledge, Eisenhower states "In a way we are reaffirming the transcendence of religious faith in America's heritage and future; in this way, we will constantly strengthen those spiritual weapons which forever will be our country's most powerful resource in peace and war."[108] Thoughts like this were commonplace after

____

[107] Ibid p 226

[108] Ibid p 226

the war, with Christian adherents in the United States being near 90%.

Trump, a Presbyterian, already aligns himself with Christian principles, and coincidentally, the Presbyterians were among the leading reformers of Protestant England in the 16th century. The Westminster Confession of Faith of 1646 acted as the joining factor for Parliamentary forces against the pro-Catholic Charles II, aligning the Protestants under a common covenant.[109] Eisenhower, likewise, was also a Presbyterian.

Other similarities between the two Presidents would be that they both had overwhelming electoral victories, both became presidents without holding any previous political office, and both are avid lovers of golf. But the most important factor that many have missed is Trump's link to Presbyterianism, and his

---

[109] https://en.wikipedia.org/wiki/Westminster_Confession_of_Faith

commitment to the Protestant core and Christian history of this country.

I once sat down with one of our senior elders of my church and asked "...how is it that the World War II generation, who were strong and determined to fight for the true principles of Christianity against Hitler's Aryanism, would come back from the war, and allow their sons and daughters to change Christian based laws (during the 1960s), sending our country towards unbelief?" And, being part of that generation, he replied (paraphrased):

"Well...after the war, there was a divide among the generation; half thought the war was necessary and good, and the other half became against the war and fighting for any future war, and this reflected in the next generation (baby boomers)."

I believe that out of anger over the damage done to families because of the war (and possibly anger against God for allowing the war), some "baby boomers" began to take liberalities that had never been taken before, and challenged Christian principles that had been in the United States since the founding of our country. There was probably a failure, in some sense, applied to the World War II generation in that after the war, they failed to come together as a community and care for the damaged families who lost loved ones. Instead they got caught up in the materialism that had occurred as a result of the reparations of the 1950s.

The baby boomers didn't want to end up in the same "war-mongering" state that their parents were born into, thus beginning an age of war protests and appeasements. Once one chooses not to fight for core beliefs, other liberalities are soon to follow. One may say "...well, if I'm not obliged to fight for my country, should I be obliged to fight for my family, let alone anything else?" Soon one loses regard to fight for anything, and seeks to be appeased by meaningless pleasures, rather than finding true joy obtained by sticking to one's principles, even if it results in hardships. The result is the changing of core principles to fit one's desires, thus to appease the mind.

What the baby boomers experienced in the 1960s is what psychologists would call "cultural" cognitive dissonance, meaning, once a group's actions start to differ from their core belief, either the actions or the belief system must be changed. As with humans, in almost all cases, the beliefs change around the desired actions. The trend of psychologists is to establish an equilibrium between the two, for the sake of the peace of mind of the group or individual.

Well...the modern psychologist has it all wrong; it is better to hold to core beliefs, deal with cognitive dissonance and allow it to exist. This establishes character and strengthens one's ability to suffer when suffering comes to play. For example, I would tell the non-believer, who has abandoned his philosophies about God; "It is better to keep apologizing to God when you do wrong, rather than to pretend God doesn't exist, and say "...I'll just do what I want.'"

The resolve of our country throughout its history, even in today's times, is solid, due to our holding to

Providentialism. Our biggest example of this in modern times would be the dropping of the atomic bomb to end World War II. As the definition would hold, "a few had to die for the sake of the many." One may not call 80,000 people "a few," but compared to the millions lost in WW II and the possibilities of many more, that number would suffice as a few.

On a smaller scale, the pre-emptive actions our military takes abroad count as Providential "moves." That small air strike or other military mission that took place, resulting in the loss of the lives of a few innocent people, was done to stop the attempt to take many lives. The media, who are generally made up of non-believers, always emphasize the "loss of innocent lives" during military maneuvers, not realizing that their own lives could be at stake without these maneuvers!

Although the number of Christian adherents in this country is high, compared to that of any other country, I believe it is more of a "nominal" figure more than one out of pure belief. In other words, probably half of those polled for the census give their religious affiliation without much thought, or simply base it on their parents or cultural identity.

My hope that by the efforts of this book, one can be awakened to the "awesomeness" that their "old style, out of date" Christian belief is really a guiding force of a nation!

Chapter Eleven

Amazing Measurements

So, there you have it. In summary, early Protestant reformers were blessed by God with technology and ingenuity, as He was pleased by their work ethic and zeal. Over time, these blessings stayed with this core group of believers, which eventually transferred to the United States, as modern England became increasingly secularized. And finally, although this concept is not easily seen, the world is "policed" essentially by "Protestant Guns," hence the subtitle of this book.

Other countries, or activist groups within our country can only "throw stones" at the establishment, because any true analysis would show that they would be defeated. Within our own country, there are organizations trying to undermine our Christian base, weaken our military and misinterpret our laws out of spite over our country's success. A lot of these organizations are funded by philanthropists, most of who believe in human empowerment over God's sovereignty.

It is ironic to me that some of these philanthropists are involved in social clubs, or "secret societies," and attempt to erase Protestant tradition, when, in actuality, these "societies" were founded out of Catholic Europe in an attempt to bring about Protestantism! For example, we learn of John Wycliffe and the Lollards in grade school, without learning who the Lollards really were- "converted" Knights of the Temple of Solomon. These knights protected Wycliffe and his followers from the various inquisitions of the Catholic Church[110], which ultimately led to the Protestant successes of the 16th century we read about earlier in this book.

I could write another book about the events that happened in the early centuries of Europe after the fall of Rome, but my main focus of this book is key events

---

[110] Robinson, John J (1989) "Born in Blood; The Lost Secrets of Freemasonry", M. Evans

that led to Protestant domination, beginning with the reign of Elizabeth I in the 16th century. The humanists, Communists, leftists, globalists and other "ists" in our modern times seem to "conveniently" forget this as they go about their own agendas. As I theorized earlier, our military "hijacked" by any of these groups would lead to implosion by their own doings, and result in an unstable world.

The final crux of this book is the brief discussion of what I believe is another underlying factor of America's success in being the "leader" of the world. This factor is overlooked or probably undiscovered, but it is a factor that must be discussed.

In writing this last part, I looked up "metric system" under a Wikipedia search, and almost immediately started to chuckle. It is obvious to read and see (in pictographs) the bias against the United States for not adopting the metric system, the only first-world country for not doing so. Immediately you are presented with a map, with the United States outlined in red (implying a negative connotation) and all the other countries (with the exception of Myanmar and Liberia) shown with a neutral grey color. Also, the wording implies America's "lacking" in the essentials of metric conversions as an outdated colloquial approach to modern times.[111]

But ironically again…this "outdated" country happens to be leading the world in all the things I listed earlier, and most importantly, in military strength. Why is it that the country that has not accepted the metric standard is the one that is "leading the world?"

In doing a quick study, I noticed the founding of the metric system occurred in a country I should have suspected from the beginning…(Catholic) France! And coincidentally, its establishment occurred exactly 100 years after the Glorious Revolution, the revolution that freed the Northern European countries from Catholic influence! Maybe there is no irony at all, and this is

---

[111] https://en.wikipedia.org/wiki/Metric_system

truly the fingerprint of God on the makings of our country, and His approval of our Protestant ways…let me explain:

During the French Revolution of 1789, Maurice de Talleyrand, a French bishop and diplomat, invited the British Parliamentarian John Riggs Miller, along with Thomas Jefferson and George Washington to work in adapting a universal form of measurements known as the metric system, but these attempts were rejected by these leaders.[112] Could it be that these British and American leaders had some foreknowledge concerning the acceptance of this system? I believe the answer is "yes," and here's why:

The history of weights and measurements had changed every couple of centuries during the middle ages of Great Britain, but in 1588, Queen Elizabeth I established a new system of measurements, known as

---

[112] Alder, Ken (2002). The Measure of all Things—The Seven-Year-Odyssey that Transformed the World. London: Abacus.

the Exchequer Standards, or Imperial Units.[113] These are (mostly) the same units that the United States still use today. Note that 1588 is also the year of the defeat of the Spanish Armada.

As we look back, John Dee wrote his *Mathematical Preface to Euclid's 'Elements'* in 1570, and his *General and Rare Memorials Pertayning to the Perfect Arte of Navigation* in 1577. After these publications, Dee was visited regularly be key Elizabethan explorers such as Sir Humphrey Gilbert, Martin Frobisher and Walter Raleigh. He was also visited at his home in Mortlake by Sir Francis Drake, vice admiral during the Anglo-Spanish war and Queen Elizabeth herself to discuss "her titles to countries in other part of the world."[114]

These shipmen listed above were privateers, and were entrusted with the secrets of the realm, taught by John Dee. It is interesting to note that Queen Elizabeth gave

---

[113] https://en.wikipedia.org/wiki/Exchequer_Standards

[114] http://www.indrakeswake.co.uk/Society/Research/dee.htm

these privateers authority to direct the Royal Navy during the Armada's invasion, under the leadership of Francis Drake. Elizabeth trusted so much in the accuracy of Dee's navigational discoveries that she was willing to allow these God-fearing men to guide the fate of Protestant England.[115]

Although it's hard to pinpoint a release of the Exchequer standards of 1588, I believe it was in response of celebration to the defeat of the Spanish Armada, although the sacred measurements were most likely given and known a decade before through the works of John Dee. It was in that year that Elizabeth authorized the perfected distance of the yard along with the proper calculations of weights. Plenty of these artifacts are on display at the Winton Gallery in South Kensington, London England, where one can see these measurements today.[116]

---

[115] https://en.wikipedia.org/wiki/Privateer

[116]

http://collection.sciencemuseum.org.uk/objects/co57528/excheq

It is likely that the American founding fathers knew the importance of these measurements, and in knowing of the successes of British navigation, and being of Protestant faith, did not want to adapt a different standard of measuring. These measurements, based off the Biblical "cubits" and other temple measurements, discovered by Dee, are still used in our country today, along with Dee's *Mathematical preface to Euclid's 'Elements'*, which is also taught in our schools today. And ironically again, the only country in the world that stuck to these "religious" measurements, is the one leading the world today!

The United States and its Allied Forces defeated Germany the Axis powers in World War II. In a general sense, the English "caliber" bullets defeated the German "millimeter" bullets. Although there are some discrepancies with this statement, most of the Allied weaponry used the English-based measurement

---

uer-standard-yard-of-queen-elizabeth-i-1588-rules-measuring-devices-linear-standards

system. The main personal carry firearm of the United States military throughout the twentieth century has been the M1911, a .45 caliber handgun also known as the Colt 45.[117]

After reviewing some of Dee's angelic communications and some of his other writings, I believe that part of the reason of America's success, and also the "pulling ahead" of the British during the age of invention, is due to the keeping of these measurements, which has honored God. Every time these measurements are used, it adds an unseen blessing upon this country, which I believe has altered history to be in America's favor. Could it be that the adaptation of the metric system be our country's final demise!?

As a carpenter, every day as I take out my tape measure to construct objects, I am humbled to know that these measurements are given to me as God's blessing through my Protestant patriarchs. And in my

---

[117] https://en.wikipedia.org/wiki/M1911_pistol

work, I am thrilled that every measurement honors my Lord, Jesus Christ, and exists as a testimony to His Providence. The "English system" of measurements is one of the most important and overlooked reasons for our successes as a Protestant country.

So…as you get in your car, fill your tank with *gallons* of gas, put *pounds* of air in your tires, drive *miles* to your job, fill your *cup* with coffee… contemplate the blessings you are inadvertently giving God each day without even realizing it! And as you sit there and enjoy uninterrupted power to your building, make purchases online with ease of commerce, plan your meetings for the day and arrive safely to your destinations…don't forget to thank the United States military presence abroad in keeping the world relatively stable!

Chapter Twelve

Donald Trump and the Presidency

Maybe this election of Donald Trump to the presidency is not a bad thing, in a sense that there will be some sort of keeping to the "old ways." It also shows that the core population of America still holds to Protestant influence, which also may not be such a bad thing. So how can we, who live in this country, "make America great again?"

The answer is easy, by maintaining the principles of Providentialism that our Protestant founders established this nation with, and by returning to the morals and beliefs given to us through God's word, the Bible. This is what was inadvertently meant by these words used in Trump's campaign, along with a return to financial stability and strength of our nations assets. Financial stability and strength can be achieved if we don't give in to supporting every cause and making concessions to groups that go against the moral principles of our roots.

Liberal leaders want to continue to move our country towards global dependence and cooperation along with establishing an "open culture," thinking that this will give us peace in an increasingly hostile world over a long period of time. What we need to do is exactly the opposite; it is better to be good stewards of our weaponry, not compromise any of our standards, be vigilant at all times and "remind" the world of our presence when necessary to stop potential conflict. As Winston Churchill once said, "An appeaser is one who feeds a crocodile, hoping it will eat him last."[118]

This last point reminds me of a meeting I had with an elderly gentleman in his late 80s one day a few years ago. The following story and conversation that was to follow went something like this:

---

[118]

https://www.brainyquote.com/quotes/quotes/w/winstonchu100130.html

I happened to stop by an office supply store a few years ago to make copies of an article for one of the deacons at my church, and I ran into a World War II naval veteran. I was on my way to the front counter to pay, and he stopped me to ask me something about ink cartridges (maybe he thought I would be knowledgeable on the matter). We got into a conversation about printing, in which he told me a little of his background of how he worked for the navy in San Francisco in the records department during World War II, and then asked me something about my copies I had just made.

I then told him that I was on my way to my church, and had to bring copies of an article for one of the deacons. He first looked surprised, then annoyed, and then remarked "...church, huh. They tried to get me into that stuff in the navy...and I wasn't having it. I was actually against the war, but I had to enlist"

Then I replied "Well... thank you for your service regardless, I'm grateful we were able to put a stop to the Axis powers."

Then he said, " Men should never have to fight, it's always wrong." So, I replied, "yeah, but it's in man's nature to fight, so maybe it's better to just figure out which side is right."

He stopped and thought for a second, then said "...do you think there will ever be a time when men won't fight?"

I smiled wryly, knowing he was much older than me and had seen many wars, and then said "...have you ever seen this happen!?" He paused and became quiet after understanding my comment about the nature of man. Then before we knew it, we were ready to checkout.

The point is that every man (or group of men) will always think they are right, and will fight for it... it is part of the pride of man. As I said earlier, we don't want to go home to our families looking like we lost! So, with a world filled with many cultures and beliefs, some are going to "lose" some are going to "win." In this case, it would be most important for each culture to seek what is right, and what is true.

Well, it seems like one could say that the Protestant culture is "winning," in terms of having the biggest weapons, and they just happen to originate from Northern European people groups who eventually cumulated in America. I refer to them as the "sons of Japheth." This is what we hear when those misinformed say: "...the world is controlled by rich elitists!" and then they epitomize Donald Trump as being the cause of this.

So, let's go back to the verses in the Bible I pointed out early in this book in Genesis 9:25-27 (NASB):

25... "Cursed be Canaan;

A servant of servants

He shall be to his brothers."

26 He also said,

"Blessed be the LORD,

The God of Shem;

And let Canaan be his servant.

27 "May God enlarge Japheth,

And let him dwell in the tents of Shem;

And let Canaan be his servant."

It may seem harsh that such a punishment could affect generations to come, but let's take a better look at what happened. After seeing his father's nakedness, Ham could of likely been joking with his brother, Shem, about the incident- similar to a lewd conversation of today. Upon hearing this news, Japheth immediately went into the tent, and covered his father. I'm sure Japheth's brothers probably taunted him after doing so, and insulted his good deed. Whatever the case may be, after hearing about this act of disrespect, Noah sought to put a curse on one of Ham's descendants, a condition on Shem's descendants, and a blessing on the descendants of Japheth.

The curse fell to Ham's son- the first being Canaan. You could interpret this to imply that sons of Ham, who eventually migrated to Africa and parts of the Middle East, who would remain behind in invention and resources throughout history. But it seems more likely that this curse refers to the location of the people group of Canaan. The land of Canaan is now known as the Southern Levant, and parts of the adjacent area.

The sons of Japheth are most likely those who crossed the Caucuses and settled in Northern Europe, and retain the cultural term, "Caucasians." These people end up settling in regions such as the British Isles, Sweden, Finland and Norway, and most of the Slavic regions.

Finally, the "tents of Shem" refers to Semitic people, such as the Arabs, or maybe even those partly of Asian descent. It also includes the Jewish people, but being of small population, they may not be included in this prophesy. Either way, Shem's "tents" could refer to either the oil of the Arab countries, or perhaps the goods produced by Asian people. Depending on the descent of the line of Shem, one could ponder this question:

Could this mean that the English/American (Japheth) were meant to be enlarged (wealth) by having the oil rich Middle East (Canaan) deal only in US currency (servants), with the main purchaser of bonds for these transactions being the Arab and Asian market (tents of Shem)?

If you interpret this verse in these sort of terms, this definitely rings true to this day. Again, it doesn't mean any one culture is better than the other in terms of physicality, but over time, some have incurred curses, and some have incurred blessings. And as far as Donald Trump, he just happens to be of Northern European descent. There is no conspiracy with "rich elitists" in this country, it's just that he feels comfortable, or "fits in" with the Protestant culture that founded this country.

So here is a man with the same descent as our Northern European founding fathers, who happened to win the election on the principle of "making America great again." He even is among the same Protestant heritage of those great reformers of the Age of Discovery. Although I'm not a politician, true greatness would include some things such as these:

- Making sure our military keeps up with technology, and properly analyzing world strategy, maintaining preemptive positioning, and securing available resources and funding.

- Preserving the core culture of the country, which is the Christian right, but allowing religious freedoms and discussion for all citizens.

- Legal reform, including restricting lawsuits in our healthcare industry, and better insurance evaluation based on health choices. Establishing or reforming laws to better protect the family. Bringing back personal responsibility by limiting frivolous lawsuits.

- Keeping tight control of our borders, including better monitoring of those here on visas.

- Maintaining good diplomatic relations, showing patience in world matters, helping countries in times of crisis, but in a reciprocal manner.

- Tax reform in a sense that all taxes levied are fair to both the poor and wealthy, and the giving of tax incentives for investing within this country.

- Prison reform in a sense of cost savings and tougher standards for repeat offenders. Also, implementing a swifter justice process in terms of capital punishment.

- Returning to tougher restrictions against vice, and similar explicit activities. Better restrictions of lewd and lascivious subject matter via the Internet. Defining gender traditionally, and helping those who struggle with their identity by coping methods, rather than allowing change.

- Not allowing federal, state or local tax support for social groups, networks, clubs or fraternities deemed hostile to our country's core Christian "right", only allowance of these groups as part of our first amendment.

Most of these philosophies I find President Trump to be aligned with, whether he as blatantly stated these policies, or supported actions directed towards these ideas. When I wrote those examples down, I myself would support even stricter standards than listed above, but I realize the difficulties of putting these pressures on the people of America, as many have become secularized. But, by heading in this direction, we will continue to have God's blessing on this country, as seen in past times.

And, well…. if you are from another country or culture, and want to concentrate all your efforts and energy into "beating" America…I will give you the simple answer on how to do it. The answer is this: Convert to Protestant Christianity, and you too can start to reap the blessings of God, and become world leaders on the stage of humanity! Because until you do so, your money and influence will be fighting against a "spiritual support system" that is much more powerful than the everyday things you see and seek to manipulate. All the money in the world can't defeat God's chosen path for those who love Him.

To those who are already part of America's Protestant core…don't sacrifice traditional standards for modern liberalities, just because you are older and "don't want to deal with any difficulties in life." Remember that the Bible says there is no age for "retirement" and we all must struggle, fight and maintain our beliefs and standards to the end… if we don't, we are in danger of angering God, and losing this blessing, which will be thrown on the next generation.

As part of being human, we tend to be short-sighted and believe that God will only punish or bless us "in the now," but we fail to realize that our actions are partly influenced by the past generation, and also that our actions will have consequence on our future generations. This is evident throughout the Bible, in verses such as these:

"You shall not worship them or serve them; for I, the Lord your God, am a jealous God, visiting the iniquity of the fathers on the children, on the third and the fourth generations of those who hate Me." (Exodus 20:5)

"…who keeps lovingkindness for thousands, who forgives iniquity, transgression and sin; yet He will by no means leave the guilty unpunished, visiting the iniquity of fathers on the children and on the

grandchildren to the third and fourth generations."
(Exodus 34:7)

"The Lord is slow to anger and abundant in lovingkindness, forgiving iniquity and transgression; but He will by no means clear the guilty, visiting the iniquity of the fathers on the children [a]to the third and the fourth generations." (Numbers 14:18)

As I stated in chapter ten (in italics), this is exactly how "America became great." Generations of Protestant believers took it upon themselves to earnestly seek God, and set the course for individual religious freedom. The Lord granted them a blessing in doing so, and it has lasted for generations upon generations up until now. I believe the baby-boomers are the first "lukewarm" generation that has come along since the founding of America, and may cause a pivotal shift in the blessings on this country.

The results of "sin," and the willingness to partake in sin, falls on the individual first, then the family, then the neighborhood, then the town...until it becomes ingrained within the whole culture. An individual can obtain salvation out of his or her culture, because salvation is for the individual, but that person will still have to live with the hardships that may exist, as a result of the previous sins of his or her culture.

Does this seem fair? How could a loving God hold things against us? Well, I think it is more than fair. Who are we to think that after we do something bad, we can just have it "tucked under the rug." It's important that we have consequences; whether you drive a brand-new Rolls Royce or an '88 Buick, consequences must fall on us all.

Finally, I want to leave you with a simple statement that goes like this:

It is better to keep apologizing to God for times when you do wrong, or "sin," rather than to just say "God doesn't exist," and then go about your own way.

This is the wisest advice I can leave you with, in the most simplistic of terms. So, as a nation, let's make sure we "apologize" every day, and seek to get right with God, so we can continue in this country's blessings!

Closing Thoughts

Part of my reason for writing this was that I was astounded by the hostilities over this past election, and thought it would be good to put things in proper perspective. Now the reader may not call my perspective "proper," but it is my hope that some of the ideas in this book would be taken to heart, and would cause one to think before one acts.

A lot of the topics in my discussion I have studied off and on over the past 20 years, so it helped me to put my thoughts together in an orderly format, such as a book. I admit that I am not a scholar on any particular issue or subject in history, but know enough to make some conclusions.

I could have expanded upon many of my subjects, but I wanted to keep this book short, making it a "quick read," because I know in this day and age, time is valuable. Hopefully this book has given you good insight into how we have ended up in our times as we know them today.

Finally, I truly do think America is great, not in a bad way, but in a good way for the reasons given in this book. I do believe we are in danger of losing this greatness, so I pray that our core Christian Right within our leadership doesn't "give in" to the pandering of the press, special interest groups, lobbyists, infiltrators, etc.

In the case of the younger generations against the Christian Right, most are misinformed and are following social trends, given over to simplicity and their own desires. As far as the older generations, some are either getting paid to thwart this nation's core, while others "think they are so smart," have lived their lives their own way in that they have come to believe it is the right way, when in fact, it is not.

But in any case, I've "said my say," made my points and "got this off my chest." It will be interesting to see where this nation is headed, as I will be watching as I go on with my daily life. Who knows what will happen, but I pray that God will continue to bless America, and that you can gain this blessing too!

Wikipedia citations:

Although Wikipedia is an ever-changing source of information, the majority of its historical articles are written by over 80,000 experts in their fields, and edited by over 30,000 contributors and staff. This makes it the largest online encyclopedia-based information sharing cite, and for quick references, a good, reliable source. The articles cited have remained unchanged over a long period of time, due to the consensus of experts on each topic. This author finds this source suitable for quick knowledge applied to a book such as this, plus it makes it easy for the reader to look it up.

Suggested Readings:

Fell Smith, Charlotte (1909). John Dee: 1527–1608. London: Constable and Company.

Robinson, John J (1989) "Born in Blood; The Lost Secrets of Freemasonry", M. Evans

Federer, William J (1994) America's God and Country; Encyclopedia of Quotations. Amerisearch, Inc. Pub

Weber, Max. (1906) The Protestant Ethic and the Spirit of Capitalism. New York: Scribner, 1958.

Guyatt, Nicholas (2007). Providence and the Invention of the United States, 1607–1876. Cambridge University Press

Flynn, David (2008) Temple the Center of Time. Anomalos Pub. House.

Nicolson, Adam (2003) God's Secretaries; The Making of the King James Bible. Harper Collins Pub.

Edwards, Brian (1976) God's Outlaw; The Story of William Tyndale and the English Bible. Evangelical Press.

Larson, Bob (2013) Curse Breaking; Freedom from the Bondage of Generational Sin. Destiny Image, Inc.

Yusuf Ali, Abdullah (2003) The Qur'an; Translation. (11th ed.) Tahrike Tarsile Qur'an, Inc.

New American Standard Bible (1960) Foundation Publications, Inc